CANNABIS COOKBOOK BIBLE

71
MEDICAL MARIJUANA
EDIBLES RECIPES

- 3 BOOKS IN 1 -

BY

MARIE SPILOTRO

Disclaimer

This book is designed to provide information about selected topics on Cannabis Edibles. Every effort was made to create this book as accurate as possible, but no warranty is implied.

The information is provided on an "as is" basis. The author shall have neither liability nor responsibility to any person or entity concerning any loss or damages arising from the information contained in this book.

The information in the following pages are broadly considered to be truthful and accurate of facts, and such any inattention, use or misuse of the information in question by the reader will render any resulting actions solely under their purview.

The information found in this book is intended for informational purposes only and should thus be considered, universal.

Contents of Book 1

21 Delightful Snacks & Hot Drinks

Contents of Book 2

27 Delightful Starters, Maincourses and Salads

Contents of Book 3

23 Delightful Cannabis Candy & Dessert

BOOK 1

21 Delightful Snacks & Hot Drinks

BY
MARIE SPILOTRO

Introduction to Edibles

With all the choices available to medical Cannabis patients nowadays, most are picking to explore methods of medicating beyond the traditional paper or pipe. Cannabis pervaded products commonly referred to as edibles, deliver additional option to patients who cannot, or rather not to smoke their Marijuana.

Edibles come in several different varieties including brownies, candy, chocolate bars, cookies, drinks, pills, snacks, spreads, and more. There are even assured companies that offer a medicated meals-on-wheels service for patients that cannot physically leave the house. Marijuana consumed orally enters the bloodstream after being digested or broken down in the belly, and is absorbed in the guts. Consumption of infused products is a healthier alternative to inhaling Marijuana smoke, because there is no exposure to carbon, tar, carcinogens, etc.

Patients, such as those on supplemental oxygen, turn to Marijuana-infused edibles while smoking is no longer a choice. In regards to patients with eating and digestive illnesses, edibles testing high in cannabidiol aka CBD are not only a great source of nausea-reducing medication, but likewise, a vital source of essential calories and nutrients. The similar is true for cancer patients suffering from nausea caused by their treatments and expecting mothers dealing with hyperemesis aka morning sickness. Additionally, most patients select edibles as their preferred technique of consumption because they have a more discreet way to medicate, while others prefer the longevity of effects while ingesting Marijuana, compared to the fast-acting results of smoking it.

First-time medical Cannabis patients typically start with a low dose of 10 to 15 mg active cannabinoids aka THC, or CBD. However, only you could determine what dosage works well for you. It often requires experimenting with different effectiveness and types of edibles.

It will be a learning procedure through many trial and errors. Retain a journal and record your experiences with various products, dosages, and attempt to distinguish what ratio of cannabinoids in what dosage provides the maximum therapeutic effect for your specific ailment or health condition.

Chapter 1 – Edible Categories

There are many varieties of edibles available on the market these days, pervaded edibles can all be split into three primary classes: those geared towards gastrointestinal uptake digested through the stomach, those geared towards oral absorption through sativa, and a few that fit into a hybrid category that targets both.

Gastrointestinal uptake

The most collective edibles are geared towards gastrointestinal absorption. Several edible where the cannabinoids are absorbed through the stomach falls into this category; this includes brownies, cookies, pill capsules, snacks, and most food varieties. These types of edibles tend to take longer to activate within the body sometimes as long as two hours but develop a longer-lasting effect up to eight hours of relief.

Oral uptake

Edibles geared towards oral absorption can distress a patient almost instantly, but tend to wear off faster within two to three hours long. Those edibles that you hold in your mouth for an extended period like suckers, tablets, and tinctures fall into this category.

Hybrids

Certain items, for instance, infused drinks and chocolate blocks, drop into a hybrid class because they are intended to be absorbed in both the mouth and the belly. These types of marijuana edibles are a middle ground between oral and intestinal absorption, proposing fast-acting aid as patients typically feel this type of edible within a half hour that can last for four hours or even more.

Edible Effects

Because most edibles are exposed to certain kind of heat during the cooking process, most of the sluggish cannabinoids such as CBDA and THCA, are transformed to THC, CBD, and CBN. This heating process, identified as decarboxylation, as well as the high levels of THC located in edibles, grind together to create an ideal treatment for most disorders, health conditions including chronic pain, muscle inflammation and spasms, autoimmune diseases, nervous system disorders, insomnia, and nausea, and they all provided the patient is well enough to ingest the medicine. The acid formulates of THC and CBD. THCA and CBDA are highly beneficial and submit their medicinal help, so finding infused edible products that are not entirely decarboxylated is desired.

While anyone can enjoy the help of edibles, patients who have Crohn's Disease, an autoimmune disorder of the gastrointestinal aka GI tract that affects as most as 700,000 Americans, find this technique of medicating extremely valuable.

It is because Crohn's Disease occurs in the GI tract, precisely where edibles distribute beneficial active and inactive cannabinoids at the origin of the problem. Ingesting Marijuana will affect you differently than smoking the plant.

However, precisely what effect edibles will have on you depends on numerous aspects: the potency and type of the edibles you are using, your tolerance, your body chemistry, and even how much you've had to eat. Since the effects of eating an edible differ significantly from the effects of smoking, most first time consumers are caught off guard by the stronger potency and long-lasting results. Despite CBD's anxiety-relieving properties, most people experience a heightened sense of anxiety and paranoia while they ingest an edible initially. It is caused by various factors but tends to mostly deal with the fact that most people are not used to ingesting Marijuana, yet and have feelings of doubt, which leads to paranoia and anxiety. It appears to fade away the more you eat them, and get used to the effects.

While you smoke Cannabis, you only obtain a small quantity of the cannabinoids in each draw, though the effects will be felt suddenly. It is unlike eating edibles, which tend to hit you much more slowly.

Most Marijuana edibles take approximately 30 minutes to 1 hour to reach maximum effect, so make sure to allow adequate time before consuming more. Eating infused treats tend to release the results in waves as the stomach processes the cannabinoids and digests over a 2 to 6 hour period.

Chapter 2 - Are edibles safe to eat?

Edible medical Marijuana is safe and won't cause any long-term toxicity. However, you may need to note while edibles industries are supposed to operate out of commercial business, ensuring all health and safety regulations, there is no entity currently in place to assure compliance with these regulations. Unfortunately, because there is no regulatory system in place to oversee edible or infused goods production, patients need to exercise caution while obtaining edibles.

Most states necessitate nothing more than a commercial cooking license to sell to a dispensary. Also, the quality of the Marijuana that is used to initialize dispensary-bought edibles is nearly impossible to determine. Certain companies utilize edibles as a way to dispose of Cannabis that else couldn't be retailed; such as buds heavily laden with spider mites or mold.

Because of this, it is very vital to get your edibles from a trusted source where lab tests their products for potency, microbiological pollutants, and learn how different terpenes affect you. Patients with severe allergies are advised to utilize extreme caution while selecting edibles, as the kitchen could be contaminated with trace of gluten, nuts, lactose, or even pet dander.

Dosing Recommendations

While selecting an edible, it is vital to pay attention to the potency of the product. This will benefit you to determine how much product you should eat, as most edibles are designed to be split into multiple quantities. The precise potency of an edible can be harsh for a patient to define, because the strength of an edible depends on the influence of the product used to infuse it.

For instance, a sweetie that comprises five grams of shake or poor superiority bud is not necessarily going to be sturdier than one that has two grams of prime quality bud. Certain manufacturers list their products in strengths such as 10x, 20x and things like that. Although these numbers benefit a bit with dosages, typically 5x per dosage, so 20x is 3 to 4 doses.

It is impossible to determine precisely how much Marijuana is in one of these products without questioning. Supplementary edible companies label their products with the amount of Marijuana that is diffused in grams. The issue with this is that, unless you distinguish how potent that gram of Cannabis was, there is no way for you to say how dominant the edible could be. The similar goes for producers who test their products for total cannabinoid content and list the number in milligrams .

These numbers can be misleading because they disregard the individual bioactive compounds entirely in the plant, things like; THCV, THC-A, CBD, CBN, etc. 10 to 15 mg of active cannabinoids like CBD or THC is naturally a decent starting point for medical Cannabis patients that are ingesting Marijuana for the first time.

30 to 100 mg of energetic cannabinoids is considered a daily dose by most patients who consume Marijuana regularly, although it will vary per specific user. Merely you, and your care provider can define what dosage works well for you.

Discovery of your ultimate ratio of cannabinoids often necessitates testing with different potencies and kinds of infused edibles though tracking your progress in a bulletin. While purchasing infused products, look for edibles that are lab tested, utilize quality components, and have correct labels on the product's packaging, including the recommended dosage.

Utilize the cannabinoid content numbers on the packaging as a rough guideline to determine your preferred dose. You may need to ask, in case the product is lab tested fact, because you do not see any apparent testing data, even though chances are the response will be what you see, is what you get.

Not ever pause to ask your bud tender about a specific product, it's their job to be educated on the subject and benefit you navigate through their wide selection of Marijuana-infused products.

They could be happy to give you advice on edibles as they interact with a lot of patients daily, giving them the ability to hear feedback from people in similar situations as yourself. First-time medical Cannabis patients typically get started with a low dose of 5 to 10 mg of THC. However, Marijuana is personalized medicine; and like I said only you could determine what dosage works best for you.

Chapter 3 – Decarboxylation Process

In case you have the extravagance of being able to attain your medicine from a legal dispensary near you, you may have seen the vast selection of edibles that are beginning to overflow the shelves.

These pre-made, pre-packaged Marijuana infused treats are more accessible to patients nowadays than ever before, but unfortunately, most edibles still come filled with sugar, very high fructose corn syrup, and other unhealthy elements.

Whereas these processed food delights can be an easy way to get medicated on the go, most medical Cannabis patients prefer making their own medicated snacks and infused meal, and for a decent purpose. Using Marijuana as medicine initiates with understanding the basic science of decarboxylation, and why it is a crucial procedure in making edibles, tinctures, and topical usages.

To get the full medicinal significance out of your Marijuana, it desires to be heated to a temperature that is just not likely to find in the human digestive structure. The major downside of decarboxylating is that the more unstable terpenes and other aromatics that give the plant its signature aroma and flavor are lost through the procedure. Tallying an equal amount of raw material to the decarboxylated materials may improve the taste and smell of your makings, but education on how to decarboxylate Marijuana from the beginning properly will save you a lot of money, time, energy and product while cooking with Marijuana.

The Decarboxylation Process

The predominant compounds located in Marijuana are THCA and CBDA. THCA is the dominant cannabinoid in Marijuana, while CBDA predominates in fiber-type hemp. CBDA and THCA accumulate in the secretory cavity of the glandular trichomes, which primarily occur in female plants and most aerial parts of the flowers.

The attentiveness of these compounds depends on the variety of Marijuana and its process, harvesting, and storage conditions. While protected in their acidic forms, CBDA and THCA are not bioavailable to the body's cannabinoid receptors. Arising either obviously within the plant, or upon decarboxylation heating the plant material, these acids are nonenzymatically decarboxylated into their equivalent neutral forms THC and CBD. THCA is not psychoactive, so it does not develop mind and body altering effects. In case you need to achieve the full psychoactive results of your butter, fats, alcohols, oils or sugars, decarboxylating the plant material to convert the THCA to THC before the infusion is vital. A resistor of heating temperatures and times is critical while cooking with Marijuana. Heating Marijuana likewise converts THC into CBN.

In about 70% decarboxylation, THC is converted into CBN at a faster rate than the THCA is transformed to THC. Sophisticated CBN levels will develop more sedative effects. Researches show cannabidiol aka CBD has a terrific medical perspective, particularly in the dealing of seizure illnesses and paediatric patients.

Symptoms likewise suggest CBD lowers blood sugar, which makes it desirable for treating diabetes. Its tranquilizing properties make it useful in the treatments of stress-related and sleep disorders. CBDA and CBD are non-psychoactive. Contrasting THCA and THC, converting CBDA to CBD won't make psychoactive merchandise. CBD has a therapeutic effect. It makes it perfect for treating youngsters, the aged or patients that favor less psychoactive effects. THC vaporizes faster than CBD, consequently decarboxylating higher CBD varieties may develop more upper CBD-enriched material. However, in case you are not consuming a high CBD strain, spreading the heating procedure may undertake no more than burning off the THC. There are much debate and opinion on this process and very little scientific evidence to establish the most critical technique. The single real way to prove the safety, consistency, and potency of your Marijuana products is to have them lab tested.

How to Decarboxylate Marijuana

Note: There will be a powerful odor of Marijuana during this process.

1. Preheat oven to 225° F or 110° C.

2. Line an oven safe dish or a rimmed baking sheet with parchment paper.

3. Break up the Marijuana buds into smaller pieces by hand, place the material in the bowl close together but not stacked on one each other, so basically less unused space, is better.

4. While the oven is pre-heated, bake for about 20 minutes to remove the dampness, but it will be depending on the freshness of the material. Also look out for the plant color while it's getting darker, basically light to medium brown shade. While it is time to remove from the oven, the material might be crumbly looking.

5. Set the plant substantial aside and pause till it is cool enough to grip. Turn the oven up to 240° F or 115° C and wait for it to heat up.

6. While the Marijuana is cooled, lightly crumble by hand and distribute evenly over the bottom of the dish.

7. Cover the bowl with an aluminum foil, folding the edges tight to seal and return to the oven. Continue baking for an additional 45 to 60 minutes for higher THC and 60 to 90 minutes for higher CBD.

8. Take out from the oven and let it cool fully, before removing the foil.

Dependent on the material you are using, it may be subtle enough and require no further processing. In case not; you could place the content in a food processor or blender, pulsing the Marijuana until it is coarsely ground. Be cautious not to over grind the material, as you do not need a super fine powder.

9. Place in a sealed container, and if you have a material made of glass, is preferred, and store in a cool, dry place.

As a side note, most recipes in this book will require you to have either; CannaMilk, Cannabutter, or Canna-Oil, therefore I will provide instructions on how to make those first.

Cannamilk ingridients:

- 1 liter of whole milk or full-fat milk
- 25 grams of your most exceptional Cannabis
- Medium saucepan
- Cheesecloth
- Metal made large mixing bowl

- Whisk or stirring spoon

Cannamilk Instructions:

1. Put a few inches of water into the medium pot, and put the water on medium temperature, bringing the liquid to a slight boil.

2. In a steel bowl, combine your Marijuana buds with your milk, and begin whisking them together. This is the fun part.

3. Decrease your boiling pot of water to low heat. Thus the liquid starts to rumble and put the steel bowl so that the bottom of the pan touches the hot water inside the vessel. This will produce a semi-double boiling effect, keeping your milk at a stabilized temperature to prevent it from curdling.

4. Make sure you keep the heat low and slow cook the milk and Cannabis to avert the THC from getting crumbling.

Mix it occasionally with your whisk, to keep the mixture combined.

5. Allow the Cannamilk to cook from a minimum of 30 minutes, up to 3 hours, subject on the strength and potency you craving. Make sure that this entire cook time is happening with a shallow heat.

6. After this prepared, strain the mixture through a cheesecloth to eliminate the buds and leaves, and pile your freshly prepared Cannamilk in the fridge for future usage.

CannaButter Instructions:

First of all, the cooking ratio: Utilize approximately 1 cup of butter for each ½ ounce of Cannabis.

1. Start with spreading your ground nuggets, jiggle or trim equally onto a baking sheet with a baking paper. Heat your oven to 240 Degrees Fahrenheit or 115 Degrees Celsius, and bake it for about 40 to 50 minutes. It will turn out very dry, but this is the result you want.

2. In a medium cooking pan, heat 1-2 quarts of water and allow this to get hot. After ready, throw in your sticks of butter, but remember; two sticks for ½ ounce grass. Retain the heat on medium-low to slowly melt the butter.

3. Subsequently, the butter has melted; add in those dank buds you just defined in the stove. Mixing it regularly, and allow it to cook on your lowest heat setting for 2½ to 3½ hours.

4. After the dough has slow cooked long enough, take a cheesecloth and place it over a bowl substantial sufficient to hold your batch of butter. Dispense the mixture over the cheesecloth and into the pan cautiously. Next, make sure that you wrap the cheesecloth and give it a squeeze to extract any remaining oil.

5. Allow the mixture to cool for about 45 minutes, and then place it in the fridge to cool a little further. While you put this THC laden concoction in the refrigerator, over time, the top layer will rise separately from the water, and remember that this is the part when you are going to peel off after it's completely separated. Make sure all extra water is scraped off and store your fresh reefer extract in a jar or air-tight container for future usage.

Canna-Oil Ingredients:

•   1-1 ½ ounces of finely ground Cannabis, buds or trim.
•   Twenty-eight ounces of cooking oil, which is always better with olive oil.

Canna-Oil Instructions:

•   First, boil your oil in the saucepan on a low to medium heat. Ensure that it doesn't boil.
•   After hot enough, drop in the 1 to 1 and a ½ ounces of excellent ground Marijuana and stir thoroughly.
•   The key here is to mix, so that the oil doesn't get too hot.
•   After you have been slow cooking the buds for about 1.5 to 2 hours, take them off the cooktop.
•   Drizzle the mixture through a cheesecloth and into the container that you will be keeping your silky Canna-mixture.
•   Put the jar of Canna-Oil in a dark place or the fridge for storage.

Now that the basics are out of our way, let get cooking!

Chapter 4 – Marijuana Stem Tea

For some of us who like to see each last bit of everything we drink, there isn't anything better than a Marijuana Stem Tea. Thankfully, Marijuana Stem Tea has been sparking up globally, consumed as a more mellow alternative to smoking Cannabis.

Sure, they won't get you quite as high as a THC-packed chunk of herb might, but these stems seem to offer pretty amazing medical help. Also, who could fight the idea of a medicinal tea-party with your contacts right?

In this chapter, I will explain to you in detail not only the possible medical uses of Marijuana Stem Tea, but also going to describe step by step how you could make this relaxing hot drink right from the comfort of your very own home. Marijuana stem tea is much like its name implies.

This dank concoction is a hot brew made from the byproduct stems left over from the Cannabis plant after the buds have been removed and most likely consumed. It is relatively simple to create, and significant batches can be steeped, in case you select to stake with your friends or throw an afternoon tea gathering. Inappropriately, it is not as simple as just crushing up the stems and throwing them in some hot water; many factors have to be taken into consideration while soaking some parts of the Cannabis plant, which is why this step by step guide comes into play.

Well, first of all, brewing Marijuana Stem Tea is rather resourceful. You would most likely be throwing those stems away anyways, and sweet grass should not go discarded.

For this motive, it is economical, because you might be able to get a bit more time spent high on your money's worth.

This formula will also appeal to those who have a difficult time smoking or inhaling Cannabis, whether it be because of personal preference or a medical disorder.

Essentially for those with asthma or other respiratory issues, having the option to drink a particular tea and get a thrill from it or even a healing break, sounds like heaven. Finally, those with certain medical conditions could help from this healing solution's actuality too.

What are the Remedial Benefits of Marijuana Stem Tea?

While Marijuana Stem Tea on its own has not been researched comprehensively, it is said it retains similar medical help, as other parts of the Marijuana herbals. Customers stated that this drink has assisted their depression, anxiety, asthma, chronic pain, body aches, migraines and headaches, autoimmune disorders, asthma, nausea, multiple sclerosis, rheumatoid arthritis, and much more. Many of us, drinking cannabinoids is a way for the body to achieve faster temporary release, taking consequence quicker than an edible would.

Ingredients:

The elements at this ratio will develop somewhere between 3 to 4 cups of tea, but in case you desire a greater quantity, multiply the numbers to your corresponding preference.

• Leftover stems from your favorite Marijuana, if possible organic ½-¼ cups worth.
• 3 cups of Purified water.
• Standard sized tea bag of your favorite non-ganja tea for added flavor 1 to 2 packs.
• A coffee filter, so it strains the dense matters from the liquid.

•   Milk, if possible non-dairy milk, about ½ cup or butter or coconut oil, ½ tablespoon of your favorite liquor, and about 2-3 teaspoons of alcohol.
•   Some grass or kief to enhance potency and THC content.

It is vital to begin by noting that it is not possible to brew Marijuana Stems deprived of an extra ingredient to bind the cannabinoids, precisely the THC, to the water. THC is not water-soluble, so H2O cannot absorb it, and without a source of fat, you will end up with Marijuana flavored hot water. This is the same reason why either alcohol or non-dairy milk or even butter or coconut oil are included in the components list. It is the source of fat for the THC to latch on to, so this ingredients are incredibly vital.

Instructions:

Step 1 - Decide whether or not you need to grind up your stems:

Indeed, think if it is best, because certain people think it makes no dissimilarity; determining whether or not to chore the stems before you start to process them, is entirely up to you.

There is not enough research showing which option is the most ideal, so just let your personal preference run wild on deciding this. In case you have defined to utilize a grinder, you will need to begin breaking down the stems now.

Step 2 - Get the water boiling.
Fill up a pot or a kettle with 3 cups of purified water, or more, if case you decided to increase the portion. If you have decided to go with the milk, non-dairy milk, butter or coconut oil route, you will need to add this ingredient in now, before you begin heating the water. In case you have defined to go the alcohol route, add it in, once the water already been boiled before, thus that the alcohol does not evaporate away, and ruin your entire lot.

Step 3 - Start the infusion process.
Here comes the exciting part – getting the grass in business. Once the water is boiling, start to stir in your Cannabis stems. Utilize the ratio described in the ingredients list. Stir continuously for about 8 to 12 minutes to ensure the stems have enough time to bind with the fat molecules. In case you have defined to add in an additional shake or kief, add these fillings along with the stems into an eco-friendly tea bag and then place it into the boiling water.

You are going to want to stir the pot continuously.

Step 4 - Strain and pour.
After the allotted time has passed, your tea will be pretty decent. Eliminate the now infused water from the stove top. In case you decided to utilize liquor, now is the time to add it in. Get your coffee filter prepared, and pour the liquid through the device and into additional pot. In case the tea bag was used earlier in the process, it merely needs to be detached, and the filtration step can be skipped.

Step 5 - Create that eccentric tea taste and start relishing.

The flavor of the Marijuana stem tea might not be all that appealing even if case you love the taste of the smokeable or culinary herb. For this reason, it may be valuable to implement an additional tea bag from your stash, maybe even an option with specific caffeine, in case this is a morning brew.

Apply one or two tea bags, then let them steep into that mixture you just strained. After the bags have soaked for their desired time, remove them, and pour the contents into a mug or teacup, and enjoy!

In case you do not feel like drinking your plain tea, there are methods to spice it up with milk, coconut milk, cream, honey, sugar, agave syrup, or even a little bit of a lemon. Just as it goes with tea that can't get you high, there are countless ways to enjoy your Marijuana Stem Tea.

Chapter 5 – Marijuana-Infused Hot Cocoa

This formula can be made vegan by choosing to prepare your cannamilk with coconut cream or coconut milk, as well as adding in a non-dairy alternative to the original technique. Also, make sure that you check, in case your dark chocolate contains dairy if you are choosing a vegan hot cocoa method.

Ingredients:

- 3 cups of non-dairy milk alternative, or standard milk
- A ½ cup of cannamilk
- A ⅓ cup of unsweetened cocoa powder
- Eight squares of 72 to 85% dark chocolate
- One teaspoon of sea salt
- A ½ cup of brown sugar
- A ⅓ cup of boiling water
- ¾ teaspoon of vanilla extract
- A ½ cup of half-and-half cream or non-dairy creamer

Instructions:

Step 1 - Mix the cocoa powder, sugar, and salt in a small bowl. In a medium saucepan on medium temperature, add your boiling water and the squares of dark chocolate.

Step 2 - Transfer the chocolate squares around until they melt into a liquid with the hot water.

Step 3 - Next, add in your dry ingredients: brown sugar, sea salt, and cocoa powder, and whisk them with the hot water and melted chocolate.

Step 4 - Blade in your 3 cups of milk or non-dairy substitute, as well as your cannamilk, half-and-half cream or non-dairy creamer.

Step 5 - Increase the heat and whisk energetically till the mix is steaming but not boiling yet. In terms of the regular milk, you'll be able to smell a slightly sweet scent after the dairy is ready.

Step 6 - Eliminate the mixture from the heat, stir in your vanilla extract, pour your hot cocoa into a mug, and enjoy!

Chapter 6 – Marijuana Chai Hot Cocoa

For those who dig spices and caffeine along with their hot chocolate, this is the picture-perfect formula. This delightful combination involves two favorite hot beverages and sufficiently of THC. This method can be made vegan by choosing non-dairy alternatives instead of milk.

Ingredients:

• 3 cups of non-dairy milk alternative, or regular milk
• A ½ cup of cannamilk
• A ⅓ cup of unsweetened cocoa powder
• ¾ teaspoon of vanilla extract
• 3 to 4 tablespoons of chai spice, ground cardamom, equal parts of ground cinnamon, ground ginger, ground nutmeg, ground allspice, and ground cloves
• Two tablespoons of maple syrup

Instructions:

Step 1 - In a small dish, combine your chai spice and unsweetened cocoa powder.

Step 2 - In a medium pot, combine the milk or non-dairy milk alternative, maple syrup, and cannamilk.

Step 3 - Add in your dry ingredients such as cocoa powder and chai spice.

Step 4 - Finally, use low to medium temperature, whisk the ingredients energetically until the mix is steaming and beginning to simmer.

Step 5 - Lastly, add in the vanilla extract, turn off the warmth, serve, and enjoy!

Chapter 7 –Bourbon and Marijuana Hot Cocoa

The medicinal twist on classic hot cocoa, crowded full of the fruity flavor of the earthy aroma of cannamilk and black cherry. In case you'd like to make this recipe vegan, choose a non-dairy alternative, instead of milk.

Ingredients:

- 3 cups of non-dairy milk alternative
- ⅛ cup of boiling water
- ½ cup of cannamilk
- Eight squares of 72 to 85% dark chocolate
- A ⅓ cup of unsweetened cocoa powder
- 4 oz. of Cherry Bourbon by Jim Beam
- A ¼ cup of brown sugar

Instructions:

Step 1 - Mix your brown sugar and cocoa powder in a mixing dish. In a medium pot, add in your boiling water and squares of dark chocolate then up the heat to medium level.

Step 2 - With a whisk, stir the chocolate around till it melts and dissolves into the boiling water.

Step 3 - Next, add in your cocoa powder and brown sugar and continue to whisk.

Step 4 - On a low to medium temperature, add your cannamilk, and milk or non-dairy alternative. Whisk energetically until the mixture is steaming but not boiling.

Step 5 - Next, take the saucepan away from the heat and set it separately.

Step 6 - Add 1 oz. of the bourbon into each cup that you intend to serve with the hot chocolate.

Step 7 - Offer the bourbon and hot chocolate a quick stir in the mug, and enjoy!

Chapter 8 – Lavender-Marijuana White Hot Cocoa

This formula is ideal for those who love a primarily herbal hot chocolate with less of the cocoa flavour.

This method is a little odd to make vegan, unless you could locate vegan white chocolate. In case you can find vegan white chocolate, make sure you select a non-dairy alternative to milk and develop your cannamilk with coconut milk or coconut cream.

Ingredients:

•   3 cups of whole milk or a non-dairy alternative
•   A ½ cup of cannamilk
•   One teaspoon of dried lavender
•   Two lime leaves - torn them in half
•   One teaspoon of lime zest
•   A ¾ cup of white chocolate chopped finely

Instructions:

Step 1 - Combine your dried lavender, milk, lime leaves, and lime zest in a medium pot.

Step 2 - On the medium temperature, beat the mixture till it becomes hot but not boiling. Next, switch off the heat and let the ingredients steep for 15 to 20 minutes.

Step 3 - Using a cheesecloth or filter, eliminate the herbs and lime particles from the milk, exhausting the mixture into another bowl, and throw the leftovers of the herbs away.

Step 4 - Put the strained milk into a medium saucepan on low heat, and this time add in the white chocolate and cannamilk.

Step 5 - Whisk the mixture energetically and prevent it from reaching a boil. After steaming but not boiling, turn off the heat.

Step 6 - Finally, pour the lavender, white hot cocoa into cups and enjoy!

Chapter 9 – Nutella Hot Cocoa with a Marijuana

Nutella is a pleasant chocolate hazelnut meal that numerous people already love. How about combining it with Marijuana-infused hot cocoa? Sounds like a dream, right? Commercial brand Nutella contains milk.

Therefore it isn't vegan-friendly, so in case you would like to make this recipe dairy-free, make sure to trail a vegan spread alike to Nutella and vegan marshmallows and add in non-dairy milk as a substitute.

Ingredients:

• 3 cups of non-dairy alternative or standard milk
• A ½ cup of cannamilk
• Six tablespoons of Nutella
• Marshmallows for garnish

Instructions:

Step 1 - First of all, use a medium pot, combine the milk or a non-dairy alternative, cannamilk, and Nutella.

Step 2 - Fix the stove on medium temperature and whisk vigorously until the liquid is steaming and hot enough, but not boiling.

Step 3 - After it reaches this point, remove it from the heat. Next, pour the hot cocoa in cups and top the cups off with marshmallows for an added garnish, and enjoy!

Chapter 10 – Grass Milk

In case sparking up first thing in the morning isn't for you – attempt to make this delicious grass milk. Either with cereal, on its own, or even in a cup of coffee. This formula is super simple, but takes infinite patience!

Ingredients:

- 6 grams of Marijuana of your selection
- 2 cups of heavy cream or whole milk
- Baking tray
- Saucepan
- Grinder
- Mesh sieve

Instructions:

Step 1 - This is expectedly one of the most straightforward recipes you will ever follow; start by turning the oven to 250°

Step 2 - Spread your Marijuana out in an even layer on a baking tray, and keep an eye on the hotness, because if it's too high, you could quickly lose potency.

Step 3 - Bake your Cannabis for around 35 to 40 minutes, checking it regularly.

Step 4 - After removing from the oven, allow the Marijuana to cool before grinding into a coarse, powdery texture.

Step 5 - Keep your Marijuana in an airtight container over two months.

Step 6 - After your Cannabis has been stored in a cold and dark area for two months, it is time to get cooking.

Step 7 - Get a medium pot and heat your milk or cream for low to medium temperature.

Step 8 - Add the Marijuana to the milk and cook gently, ensuring it does not go over 200 Celsius.

Step 9 - For about 45 minutes, retain your milk and Marijuana mixture cooking.

Step 10 - Eliminate from the heat and leave it for a further 10 minutes to rest.

Step 11 - Next, you must drain through a mesh sieve over a glass or bowl, ensuring you are cautious about extracting all the liquid and leaving behind any bits.

Step 12 - And you're done! Your milk will stay fresh in case you left it covered and refrigerated for up to 8 weeks. Enjoy!

Chapter 11 – Cannaoil

Ingredients:

- 6 grams of Cannabis
- 2 cups of oil, either olive, canola, or coconut

Instructions:

Step 1 - First of all, heat the oven to 250°F or 120°C. Spread the Cannabis out into an even layer on a baking sheet.

Step 2 - Next, bake the Cannabis, taking care not to let the Cannabis go over 250°F or 120°C and burn, but if this happens, you could lose potency.

Step 3 - Bake for about 35 to 40 minutes, then take out from the oven and cool before grinding into a coarse powder. This decarboxylated grass needs to be kept in a sealed container in a dark and cold place for up to 2 months.

Step 4 - Once the two months past, heat the oil in a medium pot over medium-low temperature.

Step 5 - Add the decarboxylated grass and start cooking, but you must ensure not to allow the temperature to go over 200°F or 93°C, for about 45 minutes.

Step 6 - Eliminate from heat then let it sit and keep it undisturbed for 10 minutes, before straining through a fine-mesh sieve set over a bowl.

Step 7 - Finally, press cautiously with a spoon to extract as much oil as possible. This cannaoil needs to be kept covered and refrigerated for up to 8 weeks.

Chapter 12 – Coconut Marijuana Oil

There are a variety of Coconut Marijuana Oil recipes that call for anywhere from ¼ ounce to 4 ounces of Marijuana per 1 cup of coconut oil. The potency of the methods on this site depends on the concentration of Marijuana in your essential ingredient. The amount of Marijuana in the recipe below is just a suggestion and can be modified according to your dosage.

Ingredients:

*   Crockpot
*   5 cups of distilled water
*   2 ounces of finely ground Marijuana
*   1 cup of organic coconut oil
*   Strainer or cheesecloth
*   Tupperware container with lid
*   Rubberband

Instructions:

Step 1 - First, you should melt 1 cup of organic coconut oil in the crockpot on the lowest setting.

Step 2 - Add 2 ounces of Marijuana and 5 cups of water while the coconut oil is melting. Mix everything.

Step 3 - Turn the crock pot on high temperature for one hour, and keep on stirring frequently.

Step 4 - Return the crock pot to a low setting. Let the blend to steep for 4 to 24 hours and stir it in each hour.

Step 5 - Turn the crockpot off. Pour the Coconut Marijuana Oil mix little-by-little slowly over the top of the cheesecloth and into the container.

Step 6 - Replicate this step as necessary to strain all of the liquid from the plant.

Step 7 - Conceal the pot and put in the fridge. Postpone overnight for the mixture to separate.

Step 8 - Eliminate the hardened coconut oil from the top, and remove the water.

Step 9 - Utilize Coconut Marijuana Oil in solid form, or meltdown as a liquid.

Chapter 13 – Grass Sugar

Ingredients:

- 3 grams of Cannabis
- 1/2 cup of high-proof alcohol
- 1/2 cup of granulated sugar

Instructions:

Step 1 - Warm the oven to 250°F or 120°C. Spread the Cannabis out into an even layer on a baking sheet.

Step 2 - Next, bake the Cannabis, taking care not to let the Cannabis go over 250°F ot 120°C and burn, but if this happens, you could lose potency.

Step 3 - Bake it for approximately 35 to 40 minutes, then remove from the oven and cool before grinding into a coarse powder. This decarboxylated grass will needs to be kept in an airtight vessel in a cool, dark place for up to 2 months.

Step 4 - Decrease the oven to 200°F or 93°C. Transfer the grass to a jar and cover with the alcohol.

Step 5 - Next, screw the top on tight and shake it in every 5 minutes for about 20 minutes.

Step 6 - Drain through a cheesecloth set over a bowl, discarding solids.

Step 7 - Mix the alcohol with the sugar and spread into an even layer in a glass 9 by 13-inch baking dish.

Step 8 - Bake it and occasionally stir it until the alcohol has evaporated, and the sugar is lightly golden.

Chapter 14 – Marijuana-Infused Vodka

Personally don't disregard mixing massive amounts of Marijuana with alcohol, however now and then a slight of the two can go together. Moreover, this formula offers the perfect equilibrium. Enjoy a Marijuana-infused cocktail that will provide you with some tremendous energetic feeling. The recommended ratio is about 3.5 grams of Marijuana per 750ml of alcohol for a safe and healthy balance equally. The reason for this is to evade any adverse effects from either alcohol or Cannabis.

Ingredients:

- Marijuana of your selection
- Vodka, but you could do it with whatever spirit you like
- An electric whipper that can tolerate heat
- A heat-proof measuring glass
- 2 Nitrous oxide chargers
- One large double boiler
- A cheesecloth
- Metal strainer
- Thermometer

Instructions:

Step 1 - Find 250ml of alcohol and pour into the whipper, then add the Marijuana into the mix.

Step 2 - Assign the nitrous charger to the whipper, release the gas and then unscrew the charger and add the second charge, then follow the same process.

Step 3 - After charged the second time, allow it to sit for a couple of minutes before opening it up.

Step 4 - Using your double boiler next, heat the water to about 200 degrees and pour the infused alcohol to the top of the double boiler.

Step 5 - Your liquid at this point could look very green, but this is normal and shows that the THC is not yet active.

Step 6 - Next, simmer the alcohol gradually at this heat, because it could take about 45 minutes and will it reduce the procedure.

Step 7 - Add spirit to bring the alcohol volume back up to its original.

Step 8 - Eliminate the pot from the heat and put to the side.

Step 9 - Utilize your heatproof measuring glass and metal strainer with the cheesecloth inside, to strain out any leftover Marijuana from your liquid.

Step 10 - In case you wish to, this is where you could add your pure spirit to refill any alcohol lost from the finished mixture.

Step 11 - Next, use the alcoholic pot-infused liquid you have just made, then add it to your favorite cocktail as the alcohol substitute, and you're ready to go. Enjoy!

Chapter 15 – Coconut Infused Marijuana Oil

When it comes to Coconut oil, it is by far one of the highest products on the market nowadays. Recently it has developed to be one of the most common superfoods and is endorsed to be used as oil while consuming raw or cooked nutrition.

Also, Coconut oil is made mainly of medium-chain fatty acids. This is because it receives its extra punch from lauric acid, aka C12, which encompasses about 50% of the total fatty acids. Coconut oil has been related to most different medical bits of help, counting accelerating healing time for injuries, bringing antioxidant properties, and averting bone loss.

This miracle oil is so frequently used, that people are adding it today to virtually anything. Because coconut oil is rich in fatty acids, it has the capability of creating a potent binding agent for Cannabinoids. It is also associated with other oils, such as Olive Oil, which contains less than 20% of saturated fat content.

Marijuana and Coconut oil is literally like a match made in heaven, and thanks to the recent research, it is now understood that Marijuana coconut oil helps are incomparable to any other

Marijuana based lubricant. Making Marijuana Oil with Coconut oil is easy. All you want is a hot stovetop particular Marijuana and obviously, coconut oil.

Ingredients:

- Double boiler
- ¼ to 1/2 ounce of quality Marijuana
- 1 cup of Organic coconut oil
- 2 to 3 feet of cooking twine
- Cheeseclothin a size of about 8" x 10" piece

Instructions:

Step 1 - Lay the cheesecloth out and place your buds on top. Buds could be distributed equally.

Step 2 - Bend in opposite ends to cover your buds. Now fold in one of the open terms, tuck, and finally roll it.

Step 3 - Tie the roll of bud with cooking string.

Step 4 - Next, fill the bottom pan of a double boiler with a few inches of water. Put the second and on top and heat to a gentle boil.

Step 5 - Next, add coconut oil and begin it to melt. Add roughly 1 cup of water, just enough so it will cover your bud packet while you place it in.

Step 6 - After all your coconut oil has melted, add your packet of buds.

Step 7 - Cook it for about 1.5 hours. After the mixture has turned green, remove the package and set aside to cool

Step 8 - The mix could form two layers; the water at the bottom and the decent stuff at the top.

Step 9 - Stab a few holes over the oil and let the water drain out completely.

Step 10 - Store in a glass container and you are done. Now have your coconut infused Marijuana oil.

Chapter 16 – Hot Cocoa with Canna Milk

Who doesn't Love having a Hot Cocoa, right? I just love making this! Keeps are energetic and if you've got a sweet tooth, it's the perfect solution. For this formula, you are going to want some Canna Milk.

Canna Milk Ingredients:

- 1 liter of whole milk, full-fat milk
- 25 grams of your most magnificent buds
- Medium saucepan
- Cheesecloth
- Large mixing bowl

Instructions:

Step 1 - In a steel mixing bowl, combine your Marijuana buds with your milk and begin whisking them together.

Step 2 - Heat a pot to a medium light until it boils.

Step 3 - Decrease your boiling pot of water to low heat and place the bowl so that the bottom of the pan touches the hot water inside the container.

Step 4 - Slow cook on little light the Milk while stirring it from time to time.

Step 5 - Allow the Cannamilk to cook from 30 minutes up to 3 hours, depending on the strength and potency you desire.

Step 6 - After ready, strain the mixture through a cheesecloth to remove the excess leaves and buds, and store in the fridge.

Hot Cocoa Ingredients:

- 1/3 cup of unsweetened cocoa powder
- 3/4 cup of white sugar
- One pinch of salt
- 1/3 cup of boiling water
- 3 cups of standard milk
- 1/2 cup of half-and-half cream
- 3/4 teaspoon of vanilla extract
- 1/2 cup of cannamilk

Instructions:

Step 1 - Combine the sugar, cocoa, and pinch of salt in a pot.

Step 2 - Mix it in the boiling water, and bring this combination to an easy boil while you are stirring it.

Step 3 - Remember to mix, as you need a beautiful texture. The whole process could be around 2 minutes and ensure it doesn't scorch.

Step 4 - Stir in 1/2 canna milk and 3 cups of milk, then heat it till it gets very hot, but do not boil it.

Step 5 - Eliminate from heat and add vanilla.

Step 6 - Pour into a few cups. Add the cream into the mugs of cocoa to calm it until it gets to drinking temperature and enjoy!

Chapter 17 – Marijuana-Infused Honey

The practice of adding Cannabis to honey is thousands of years old. It is broadly believed that the ancient Egyptians used a Marijuana honey recipe through rituals where they honored their deities.

There are many Marijuana-infused honey recipes obtainable, but I am about to show you one of the easiest of them all. The first thing you have to do is that you have to decarboxylate your Marijuana to transform the THCA into THC. In case you fail to do this, all you are basically doing is adding plant matter to the honey, and you're doubtful to experience much of a high.

Instructions:

•   First and foremost, preheat your oven to 240 degrees Fahrenheit and put your herb on a baking sheet in a thin layer. This is to keep the temperature reasonably low to preserve as most cannabinoids and terpenes as possible. After you get into the 320+ degree range, a fair percentage of grass's unusual compounds begin to vaporize.

• Bake the Cannabis for at least 40 minutes. By the way, I know that certain people cook their grass for up to an hour at this low temperature. Ensure you stir the Marijuana and rotate the sheet a few times during the process, or else it won't cook evenly.

• After the precious grass is decarbed and ready for action, you could add it to your honey.

Ingredients:

• A crockpot
• At least 15 grams of decarboxylated grass
• Two cups of organic honey
• A cheesecloth
• A piece of string
• A glass jar with a lid

Marijuana Honey Instructions:

Step 1 - Wrap the grass in cheesecloth and tie it with the string.

Step 2 - Put the cheesecloth in the glass jar, and pour in two cups of honey.

Step 3 - Put the jar in your crockpot, and pour enough water in the pot so that its level is above that of the baby, but not submerging the entire jar.

Step 4 - Put the lid on your pan, set the temperature to low, and cook it for 8 hours.

Step 5 - It is vital to check the pot every few hours to make sure there isn't too much pressure on the container.

Step 6 - Open the lid sometimes slightly for a few seconds.

Step 7 - Turn off the pot after 8 hours and allow the honey to cool. It is most likely best to remove the extremely hot jar from the cooker at this point, and please but be careful.

Step 8 - After the honey is ready, remove the cheesecloth from the pot and squeeze out as much amber nectar as possibly can, in order to not waste any. I endorse steeping the cheesecloth in water to create a delightful and intoxicating tea.

Step 9 - Store the jar, containing the Marijuana-infused honey in the refrigerator.

The potential helps of Marijuana-infused honey depend on what you are infusing the honey with. A high THC batch could help as follows:
- Enhance mood
- Boost appetite
- Reduce nausea and vomiting
- Aid restful sleep in case you have insomnia
- Relax the muscles
- Alleviate chronic pain

Of course, it will ensure you get high too, and while this is often a decent thing for patients with medical problems, it means you can't have it before going to work.

In most states, you could be fired from your job for submitting a positive drug test, even if you have a medical Cannabis card. When it comes to CBD honey is non-intoxicating, which means it will not show up on a drug screening unless it contains THC. A decent CBD honey can provide you with the following benefits:
- Reduction in paranoia
- Helps combat depression
- Alleviates anxiety
- Counteracts THC's psychoactive effects
- Reduces or even prevents seizures
- Reduces inflammation

•   Helps to slow down neurodegenerative disorders

In other words, with CBD canna-honey you could get all the help of edibles, and you could determine the potency of your extract. Marijuana honey can be used in numerous ways. For example, you could add it as a sweetener to hot or cold drinks, spread it on toast, or even utilize it as a glaze while grilling meat or vegetables.

When it comes to Cannabis infused honey, you have to deliberate the age-old question: Is it better to have it homemade, or is it okay to rely on dispensary-bought substances? The increasing legality of Cannabis coupled with the process of state-backed dispensaries that need to observe strict rules, means that customers no longer have to worry about the quality of the edibles they purchase.

Making Marijuana honey for example, requires grass, honey, a crockpot, and a couple of tools located in most kitchens in the US. The main reason to consider homemade Marijuana honey is economical. As a rule, cannabis edibles are very costly, so you could save yourself a small wealth in the long run by choosing for indigenous varieties.

Chapter 18 – Marijuana Peanut Butter

To successfully develop your Marijuana peanut butter bites, you'll want to start by fetching your ingredients. This recipe requires cannabutter as the grassy ingredient of choice. If you aren't sure how to make cannabutter, don't fret, this simple and easy-to-follow recipe can help. After you've rounded up your ingredients, follow the necessary steps.

Marijuana Peanut Butter Ingredients:

- 1 cup of smooth peanut butter
- 1 cup of unsalted cannabutter
- 1/4 tsp of salt
- 1tsp of vanilla
- 1 lb of powdered sugar

Instructions:

Step 1 - Line the bottom and sides of an 8×8 pan with baking paper or spray it with non-sticky oil.

Step 2 - Melt in a microwave bowl your peanut butter, cannabutter, and salt.

Step 3 - Mix until you see an even consistency, and any chunks have been divided up.

Step 4 - Stir in your vanilla and powdered sugar.

Step 5 - After you get a smooth mixture, spread it in the pan and place in the fridge until is cold.

Step 6 - After the mixture has hardened, cut it into squares, and serve and enjoy!

As you see the process is very simple. It only requires five ingredients and few steps to make Marijuana peanut butter that taste pretty spectacular.

Chapter 19 – Peanut Butter Bars Second Version

Do you ever get that feeling, that you crave something sweet, that will take you off the edge? Well, there is nothing better than jazzing up your afternoon with a cup of coffee and a few Peanut Butter Bars, so I highly recommend you to check out this formula. One thing I should mention, is that you must make sure you have some cannaoil ready before get going.

CannaOil Ingredients:

- 1-1 ½ ounces of fine Cannabis, trim or buds
- 30 ounces of cooking oil

Canna Oil Instructions:

Step 1 - Boil your oil in a pan on low light. Ensure you bring it to a slight boil.

Step 2 - After hot, drop in the 1-1 ½ ounces of Cannabis and stir. Attempt to reach a smooth mixture. The vital thing to remember while making Canna Oil is to mix it thoroughly to avoid burning the oil.

Step 3 - After you've been cooking the dough for about 1.5 to 2 hours, then take them off the stove.

Step 4 - Next, pour the mixture into a jar through a cheesecloth.

Step 5 - Place the pot of Canna Oil in a dark place or the fridge for storage

Peanut Butter Bars Ingredients

- 1 cup of melted butter or margarine
- 2 cups of cracker crumbs
- 2 cups of confectioners sugar
- 1 cup of peanut butter
- 1 and a 1/2 of cups semisweet chocolate chips
- Four tablespoons of peanut butter

Instructions:

Step 1 - In a medium bowl, mix the butter or margarine, the cracker crumbs, confectioners sugar, 1 cup of peanut butter and two tablespoons of CannaOil.

Step 2 - Mix it all till everything gets a smooth texture and is well mixed.

Step 3 - Pour into an ungreased pan and press evenly so that it is all flat at the bottom of the pan.

Step 4 - Next, you must melt the chocolate chips with the peanut butter in the microwave and stir thoroughly to get a sweet smooth paste.

Step 5 - Spread the dough over the prepared crust. Keep it cold for at least one hour before cutting into squares, and enjoy!

Chapter 20 – Grass Style Tacos

I just love Tacos, don't you? Well imagine having those cravings, but you can't be concerned to leave the flat. You could even jazz it up and turn those plain old Tacos into some Grass Style Bites right?

Ingredients

- 3 pounds of flank steak
- 1/3 cup of white vinegar
- 1/2 cup of soy sauce
- Four cloves of minced garlic
- Two juiced limes
- 1/2 cup of olive oil
- A teaspoon of salt
- One teaspoon of ground black pepper
- One teaspoon of ground white pepper
- One teaspoon of garlic powder
- One teaspoon of chili powder
- One teaspoon of dried oregano
- One teaspoon of ground cumin
- One teaspoon of paprika
- One chopped white onion
- 1/2 cup of chopped fresh cilantro
- One juiced lime
- Two large chopped tomatoes

- Two chopped jalapeno peppers
- One quartered white onion
- Four cloves of peeled garlic
- Dried New Mexico chile pods
- One pinch of salt and pepper to taste
- One package of corn tortilla
- Two cups of grated cotija cheese
- Two limes, cut into wedges
- Cannaoil

Instructions:

Step 1 - First of all, warm up your oven to 450 degrees Fahrenheit.

Step 2 - In a beautiful size bowl, whisk together the vinegar, soy sauce, four cloves of garlic, olive oil and juice of two limes.

Step 3 - Add to the mixture black pepper, salt, white pepper, chili powder, garlic powder, oregano, paprika, and cumin.

Step 4 - Next, pour the sauce over the flank steak that is laying in a bowl. Conceal both sides of the steak and leave to marinate for a couple of hours.

Step 4 - In another bowl or the same one in case you don't mind washing it, stir together the cilantro, one chopped white onion, and the juice of 1 lime. Put this aside, because you'll want this later.

Step 5 - Heat your skillet to medium-high temperature. Next, toast chile pods in the skillet for a couple of minutes, then eliminate to a bowl of water to soak for around 30 minutes.

Step 6 - Place the tomatoes, one onion, jalapenos, and four cloves of garlic on top of a baking sheet.

Step 7 - Next, roast in the oven for about 20 minutes, till toasted.

Step 8 - Put the roasted vegetables, and soaked chile pods into a blender or food processor along with salt and pepper. Shred until smooth.

Step 9 - Heat a mix of your vegetable and canna oil in a large skillet over medium-high temperature.

Step 10 - Scratch the marinated flank steak into strips. Next, cook till most of the liquid has evaporated. Don't overcook the meat, because you don't need it to be too dry.

Step 11 - Position two or three tortillas on a plate, and lay a generous amount of beef over them.

Step 12 - Next, top with a sprinkle of the onion relish and a large spoonful of the pureed salsa, and finally, add as much cheese as possible can.

Step 13 - Serve and enjoy!

Chapter 21 – Homemade Canna Popcorn

In the course of icy weather, there is nothing better than catching a movie in, with some great snacks. Here is the Homemade Canna Popcorn formula that you will love. It's easy to make, and packed with some devoted elements that will make you think you're watching a 4D picture. Once you've finished making the popcorn, kick back and relax watching your favorite movie.

CannaButter Instructions:

First of all, the cooking ratio: Utilize approximately 1 cup of butter for each ½ ounce of Cannabis.

Step 1 - Start with spreading your ground nuggets, jiggle or trim equally onto a baking sheet with a baking paper.

Step 2 - Heat your oven to 240 Degrees Fahrenheit or 115 Degrees Celsius, and bake it for about 40 to 50 minutes. It will turn out very dry, but this is the result you want.

Step 3 - In a medium cooking pan, heat 1-2 quarts of water and allow this to get hot.

Step 4 - After ready, throw in your sticks of butter, but remember; two sticks for ½ ounce grass. Retain the heat on medium-low to slowly melt the butter.

Step 5 - Subsequently, the butter has melted; add in those dank buds you just defined in the stove.

Step 6 - Mixing it regularly, and allow it to cook on your lowest heat, setting it for 2½ to 3½ hours.

Step 7 - After the dough has slow cooked long enough, take a cheesecloth and place it over a bowl substantial sufficient to hold your batch of butter.

Step 8 - Dispense the mixture over the cheesecloth and into the pan cautiously.

Step 9 - Next, make sure that you wrap the cheesecloth and give it a squeeze to extract any remaining oil.

Step 10 - Allow the mixture to cool for about 45 minutes, and then place it in the fridge to cool a little further. While you put this THC laden concoction in the refrigerator, over time, the top layer will rise separately from the water, and remember that this is the part when you are going to peel off after it's completely separated. Make sure all extra water is scraped off and store your fresh reefer extract in a jar or air-tight container for future usage.

Canna PopCorn Ingredients

- Three tablespoons of peanut oil
- One tablespoon of butter
- One tablespoon of Cannabutter
- 1/2 cup of unpopped popcorn
- 1/2 teaspoon of salt

Instructions:

Step 1 - Warm the peanut oil in a 2 to 3-quart pot over medium-high temperature.

Step 2 - Pour in popcorn sprinkle salt and kernels to cover them carelessly.

Step 3 - Add the Cannabutter and butter to the pan and cover with the lid.

Step 4 - After the kernels begins to pop, jiggle the pan back and forth. This will slow down the popping and avert you from burning parts of the popcorn.

Step 5 - Once the pops are about 2 seconds spaced out, eliminate from the heat and pour into a serving dish.

Step 6 - Taste, and add salt if preferred. Enjoy!

Chapter 22 – Jalapeno CannaPoppers

This isn't just tasty but super laid-back to create it too.

Ingredients:

- Ten jalapeno peppers, seeded and halved
- 1 cup of CannaCream Cheese, softened at room temperature
- 1 cup of shredded cheese
- A ¼ cup of bacon bits
- ¼ teaspoon of paprika
- Salt and pepper
- A ½ cup of milk
- A ½ cup of flour
- A ½ cup of seasoned bread crumbs
- Frying oil

Instructions:

Step 1 - Combine into a beautiful blend the CannaCream Cheese, paprika, salt, pepper, and bacon bits.

Step 2 - Then fill the prepped jalapeno halves with the cheese mixtures.

Step 3 - In separate bowls, set the milk, flour and bread crumbs aside.

Step 4 - Dip each jalapeno into the milk and into the flour, then lastly into the breadcrumbs.

Step 5 - Fix apart and let it dry for around 10 minutes.

Step 6 - Fry the jalapenos for around 2 minutes on each side till it gets brown. Finally, put them on a paper cloth to drain, serve, and enjoy!

Chapter 23 – Marijuana Spring Rolls

If you are hosting a party or just having a couple of friends over for a movie, these can be a picture-perfect way to get high. It is a veggie formula for those who prefer to stay strictly herbal, therefore enjoy.

Ingredients:

- Eight pieces of Rice roll papers
- One grated Beet
- One red, one orange and one yellow sliced bell pepper
- ½ Pineapple, cut into strips
- 1 Large bunch mint leaves
- 1 Large bunch cilantro, cut from stems
- 1 Bunch chopped green onions
- 8 Ounces cooked rice, nuts or tofu

Peanut Sauce Ingredients:

- A cup of natural peanut butter
- 3 Tablespoons of soy sauce
- 2 Tablespoons of sriracha sauce
- 2 Tablespoons of grated ginger
- 1 Tablespoon of lime juice

- 2 Tablespoons of Marijuana honey
- 1 Tablespoon of vinegar
- 9 Tablespoons of hot water

Instructions:

Step 1 - This formula necessitates some Marijuana honey! To create the sauce, mix all the ingredients in a dish, without the water.

Step 2 - After assorted, gradually add the hot water a bit at a time, stir thoroughly until the liquid becomes see-through.

Step 3 - Taking the rice paper, plunge it into a container of warm water, and leave it for around 15 seconds, until it become softer.

Step 4 - Supplement all the veg and fresh herbs along with any other favored components, and put into the center of the rice paper.

Step 5 - Next, roll the paper up and twist at the ends to cover the mix. Serve and Enjoy!

BOOK 2

27 Delightful Starters, Main courses and Salads

BY
MARIE SPILOTRO

STARTERS & SALADS

Chapter 1 - Herb-Infused Grilled Cheese

Once you decide that you are going to grill some of your favorite cheese and bread you love and add a little extra sparkle to it, you just going to love that don't you think? You have yourself a real fried sandwich that is bound to consume your mind and body with chill times and great vibes. It's straightforward to begin, but you want to get ahold of some Canna-Oil. In case you could 't purchase any, here's how You could make your own. This formula creates a large batch so that you could utilize this top grade medicine for all your future Cannabis recipes:

Canna-Oil Ingredients:

•   1-1 ½ ounces of finely ground Cannabis, buds or trim.
•   Twenty-eight ounces of cooking oil, which is always better with olive oil.

Canna-Oil Instructions:

•   First, boil your oil in the saucepan on a low to medium heat. Ensure that it doesn't boil.

- After hot enough, drop in the 1 to 1 and a ½ ounces of excellent ground Marijuana and stir thoroughly.
- The key here is to mix so that the oil doesn't get too hot.
- After you have been slow cooking the buds for about 1.5 to 2 hours, take them off the cooktop.
- Drizzle the mixture through a cheesecloth and into the container that you will be keeping your silky Canna-mixture.
- Put the jar of Canna-Oil in a dark place or the fridge for storage.

Ingredients:

- Six tablespoons of Marijuana Oil
- Eight slices of your favorite bread (we recommend sourdough or whole wheat)
- Eight bread sized thin cut slices of your preferred cheese (we recommend swiss or sharp cheddar)
- Fresh cut tomato slices
- Freshly picked basil leaves

Instructions:

For every grilled cheese you create, utilize one tablespoon of Canna-Oil to heat up in the pan, and a ½ tablespoon of Canna-Oil to dispense into the center of your toasts. In total, add 1½ tablespoons of ganja for each of your sandwiches.

Step 1 - Add one tablespoon of Canna-Oil into a hot skillet and place your first two pieces of bread into the Canna-Oil. Let the bread crisp, fry in the oil, and after it begins to brown to some extent, complement your slices of cheese onto your pieces of bread.

Step 2 - The cheese will start to melt, therefore get your tomatoes and basil prepared. Adorn your grilled cheese with these two components, and dispense a little Canna-Oil onto the pieces of bread before closing off the toasts.

Step 3 - Combine the two slices of crispy bread to close off the sandwich and serve for a delightful meal that will get you fried any time of day.

Step 4 - Repeat these same steps three more times to create four Herb Pervaded Grilled Cheeses.

Step 5 - Serve and Enjoy!

Chapter 2 - Easy Broccoli Grass Quiche

This formula will take you around 20 minutes to complete, yet it is well worth it. It is the perfect side dish and will leave you with a taste for more. So here is the formula you can follow, but first you are going to want some CannaButter.

CannaButter Instructions:

First of all, the cooking ratio: Utilize approximately 1 cup of butter for each ½ ounce of Cannabis.

1. Start with spreading your ground nuggets, jiggle or trim equally onto a baking sheet with a baking paper. Heat your oven to 240 Degrees Fahrenheit or 115 Degrees Celsius, and bake it for about 40 to 50 minutes. It will turn out very dry, but this is the result you want.

2. In a medium cooking pan, heat 1-2 quarts of water and allow this to get hot. After ready, throw in your sticks of butter, but remember; two sticks for ½

ounce grass. Retain the heat on medium-low to slowly melt the butter.

3. Subsequently, the butter has melted; add in those dank buds you just defined in the stove. Mixing it regularly, and allow it to cook on your lowest heat setting for 2½ to 3½ hours.

4. After the dough has slow cooked long enough, take a cheesecloth and place it over a bowl substantial sufficient to hold your batch of butter. Dispense the mixture over the cheesecloth and into the pan cautiously. Next, make sure that you wrap the cheesecloth and give it a squeeze to extract any remaining oil.

5. Allow the mixture to cool for about 45 minutes, and then place it in the fridge to cool a little further. While you put this THC laden concoction in the refrigerator, over time, the top layer will rise separately from the water, and remember that this is the part when you are going to peel off after it's completely separated. Make sure all

extra water is scraped off and store your fresh reefer extract in a jar or air-tight container for future usage

Ingredients:

- One tablespoons of Butter
- One tablespoon of CannaButter
- One teaspoon of minced garlic
- 2 cups of chopped fresh broccoli
- 1 unbaked pie crust
- 1 and a 1/2 cups of shredded mozzarella cheese
- Four well beaten eggs
- 1 and a 1/2 cups of milk
- One teaspoon of salt
- 1/2 teaspoon of black pepper
- One tablespoon of melted butter

Instructions:

Step 1 - Heat the oven to 350 F or 175 degrees C.

Step 2 - Over low heat, melt your butter and Cannabutter in a large saucepan.

Step 3 - Add onions, garlic, and broccoli. Stir it while you cook it till all the components are soft.

Step 4 - Spoon vegetables into crust and shake it with some cheese.

Step 5 - Combine the eggs and milk, and flavour according to your taste with salt and pepper. Stir in the melted butter, and pour your egg mixture over the cheese and vegetables.

Step 6 - Finally, bake it in a warmed up oven for about 30 to 50 minutes.

Step 7 – Serve and enjoy right out of the oven!

Chapter 3 - Marijuana Quinoa Salad

I am already convinced that you will love to cook this formula, which is specifically tailored to be gluten-free, containing delicious flavors of crisp, matured tomato, cucumber, parsley, fluffy quinoa and the most magnificent of all, some Cannabis.

This formula is good for six servings and only takes about 30 minutes to prepare and cook.

Ingredients:

- 1 cup of dry quinoa grain
- One clove minced garlic
- Two tablespoons of fresh lemon juice
- ¼ cup of Canna-Oil
- ¼ cup of extra virgin olive oil
- One large cucumber
- 1 pint of cherry tomatoes
- ⅔ cup of chopped parsley
- ¼ cup of chopped mint
- One scallion
- Salt and black pepper
- A splash of gluten free soy sauce

Canna-Oil Ingredients:

• 1-1 ½ ounces of finely ground Cannabis, buds or trim.
• Twenty-eight ounces of cooking oil, which is always better with olive oil.

Canna-Oil Instructions:

• First, boil your oil in the saucepan on a low to medium heat. Ensure that it doesn't boil.
• After hot enough, drop in the 1 to 1 and a ½ ounces of excellent ground Marijuana and stir thoroughly.
• The key here is to mix so that the oil doesn't get too hot.
• After you have been slow cooking the buds for about 1.5 to 2 hours, take them off the cooktop.
• Drizzle the mixture through a cheesecloth and into the container that you will be keeping your silky Canna-mixture.
• Put the jar of Canna-Oil in a dark place or the fridge for storage.

Instructions:

Step 1 - Fill a medium pot with 1¾ cups of water and pour in your 1 cup of dried quinoa grain. Complement in a splash of olive oil and a pinch of salt, and turn the stove up to medium heat.

Step 2 - After the water has begun boiling, allow the quinoa to keep on cooking for roughly 10 minutes or till all the water has vanished and the quinoa is soft and steaming.

Step 3 - When the quinoa is getting cooked, you should chop your vegetables and herbs. Attempt to slice everything into smaller, less than bite-size pieces, for the ease of consumption

Step 4 - Get a medium sized container and arrange your sauce now. Add in a ¼ cup of Canna-Oil, ¼ cup olive oil, two tablespoons of lemon juice, one clove of minced garlic, cracked pepper and a splash of gluten free soy sauce. Whisk these ingredients together until all combined.

Step 5 - Grab a crisp and a bigger serving bowl. Complement the quinoa and the chopped vegetables to this dish, then pour the freshly whisked ganja sauce over it.

Step 6 - Fold the quinoa, seasoning, and veggies with the spoon to evenly distribute the Marijuana. Serve and enjoy!

Pasta Dishes

Chapter 4 - Smoky Mac N Cheese

Measured as a definitive in ease of food, mac n cheese is a household favorite across the US. This unique style Marijuana Infused Mac N Cheese will definitely give you a serious blow!

Ingredients:

- ½ Cup of cold cannabutter plus one tablespoon of melted cannabutter
- ½ Unsalted butter
- 1 Cup of Flour
- 4 Cups of milk
- 2 Teaspoons of salt
- ¼ Teaspoon of cayenne pepper
- 1 Teaspoon of black pepper
- 1 Pound of penne pasta
- 1 Cup of shredded smoked mozzarella
- 1 Cup of shredded cheddar cheese
- 1 Cup of shredded American or Swiss cheese
- ¾ Cup of grated parmesan cheese
- ¼ Cup of breadcrumbs

Instructions:

Step 1 - Heat your oven to 350 degrees to get going.

Step 2 - Mix and melt both; the cannabutter and regular butter over medium heat in a large pot.

Step 3 - After they are melted, whisk in the flour and keep whisking and mixing until cooked, usually around 4 to 5 minutes.

Step 4 - In a separate medium-sized pot, boil the milk over high temperature.

Step 5 - After boiling it, add the hot milk to the butter and flour mixture, whisking in to ensure that they are appropriately mixed.

Step 6 - Add in some salt, black pepper, and cayenne pepper, then continue to cook until the entire mixture is boiling.

Step 7 - After it has reached the boiling level, eliminate from the heat and stir in the already cooked penne pasta and all the cheeses, and around a ¼ cup of Parmesan cheese to sprinkle on the top of it.

Step 8 - Dispense the pasta mixture into a greased baking plate, and mix the breadcrumbs with the remaining cheese, and add in 1 tablespoon of melted cannabutter to the mix.

Step 9 - Shake the blend on the top of the pasta, and bake it for 30 to 40 minutes until it gets golden brown.

Step 10 - Serve and enjoy!

Chapter 5 - Italian Garlic Cheese Pasta

Who doesn't desire a large bowl of carbs while they are smoking a bit of Marijuana, right? Well, why not endeavor something similar in a form of edibles right? This formula is called the Italian Garlic Cheese Pasta is of course infused with Marijuana and will serve about 4 to 6 people, and on the top of that, it will only take ten minutes to create it.

Ingredients:

*   Your selection of pasta - try decent quality if possible
*   Salt and pepper
*   Four tablespoons of cannabutter
*   Seven cloves of chopped garlic
*   ¾ cup of parmesan cheese
*   Large skillet
*   Large saucepan

Instructions:

Step 1 - First, melt your cannabutter over a large skillet on medium temperature.

Step 2 - Complement the garlic to the butter, and cook it till a light golden brown color is visible.

Step 3 - Eliminate the pan from the heat and put it on the side.

Step 4 - Bring a huge pot of salted water to the boil and add your pasta in.

Step 5 - Cook it until is soft, and then drain away from the pasta water, leaving around ½ cup behind for later.

Step 6 - Put the pasta back into your pot with the last of the pasta water, then enhance in the garlic infused cannabutter some pepper and salt.

Step 7 - Mix all the components well and finish with a topping of parmesan cheese.

Step 8 – Serve and enjoy!

Chapter 6 - Spaghetti Bolognese

You might be aware that spaghetti bolognese is frequently voted as one of the top ten dishes. Nevertheless, for this formula, you are going to want some Canna-Oil.

Canna-Oil Ingredients:

• 1-1 ½ ounces of finely ground Cannabis, buds or trim.
• Twenty-eight ounces of cooking oil, which is always better with olive oil.

Canna-Oil Instructions:

• First, boil your oil in the saucepan on a low to medium heat. Ensure that it doesn't boil.
• After hot enough, drop in the 1 to 1 and a ½ ounces of excellent ground Marijuana and stir thoroughly.
• The key here is to mix so that the oil doesn't get too hot.
• After you have been slow cooking the buds for about 1.5 to 2 hours, take them off the cooktop.

- Drizzle the mixture through a cheesecloth and into the container that you will be keeping your silky Canna-mixture.
- Put the jar of Canna-Oil in a dark place or the fridge for storage.

Ingredients:

- 1/2 tbsp of olive oil
- 1/2 tbsp of Canna-Oil
- Four finely chopped smoked bacon
- Two finely chopped medium onions
- Two trimmed and finely chopped carrots
- Two finely chopped celery sticks
- Two finely chopped garlic cloves
- 500g of beef mince
- 2 x 400g tins of plum tomatoes
- A small pack of basil leaves
- 1 tsp of dried oregano
- Two fresh bay leaves
- 2 tbsp of tomato puree
- One beef stock cube
- One seeded and finely chopped red chili
- 125ml of red wine
- Six cherry tomatoes sliced in half

- 75g of grated Parmesan
- 400g of spaghetti
- ¾ finely chopped garnish

Instructions:

Step 1 - Put a large saucepan on medium temperature and add your oil and canna-oil.

Step 2 - Next, fry the bacon for around 10 mins, until it is crispy.

Step 3 - Decrease the heat and add the onion, garlic, carrot, and celery. Stir them until everything softens.

Step 4 - Rise to medium temperature and add the mince.

Step 5 - Fry till the meat is brown color everywhere.

Step 6 - Next, add the chopped basil, tinned tomatoes, bay leaves, oregano, tomato puree, stock cube, chili, cherry tomatoes, and wine.

Step 7 - Stir it carefully and bring to a boil and reduce the heat to a simmer. At this point, cook it while is covered for just over an hour.

Step 8 - Add parmesan to thicken the mixture.

Step 9 - Now, cook the spaghetti as to the pack instructions commands.

Step 10 - Put the cooked pasta on a plate and cover the top with your mince sauce.

Step 11 - Serve and enjoy!

Chapter 7 – Canna Macaroni & Cheese

Imagine when you come home from work, and all you want to do is kick back in front of the telly and have some Macaroni & Cheese Pasta. Well, this formula will take you 30 mins to create, but I promise it will worth it. Before you get going, let's jump straight to the most important part – The CannaButter. Obviously in case you have some available, then skip this step.

CannaButter Instructions:

First of all, the cooking ratio: Utilize approximately 1 cup of butter for each ½ ounce of Cannabis.

1. Start with spreading your ground nuggets, jiggle or trim equally onto a baking sheet with a baking paper. Heat your oven to 240 Degrees Fahrenheit or 115 Degrees Celsius, and bake it for about 40 to 50 minutes. It will turn out very dry, but this is the result you want.

2. In a medium cooking pan, heat 1-2 quarts of water and allow this to get hot. After ready, throw in your sticks of butter, but remember; two sticks for ½ ounce grass. Retain the heat on medium-low to slowly melt the butter.

3. Subsequently, the butter has melted; add in those dank buds you just defined in the stove. Mixing it regularly, and allow it to cook on your lowest heat setting for 2½ to 3½ hours.

4. After the dough has slow cooked long enough, take a cheesecloth and place it over a bowl substantial sufficient to hold your batch of butter. Dispense the mixture over the cheesecloth and into the pan cautiously. Next, make sure that you wrap the cheesecloth and give it a squeeze to extract any remaining oil.

5. Allow the mixture to cool for about 45 minutes, and then place it in the fridge to cool a little further. While you put this THC laden concoction in the refrigerator, over time, the top layer

will rise separately from the water, and remember that this is the part when you are going to peel off after it's completely separated. Make sure all extra water is scraped off and store your fresh reefer extract in a jar or air-tight container for future usage.

Ingredients:

- ½ pound of elbow macaroni
- One tablespoon of canola oil
- One teaspoon of salt
- For cheese sauce
- Five tablespoons of cannabutter
- ½ cup of all-purpose flour
- 2½ to 3 cups of warm milk
- 4 ounces of grated smoked mozzarella
- 8 ounces of medium grated cheddar
- One teaspoon of kosher salt
- One teaspoon of smoked paprika
- ½ teaspoon of fresh ground black pepper
- ½ teaspoon of ground nutmeg
- 1 cup of breadcrumbs

Instructions:

Step 1 - First of all, heat your oven to 375 degrees temperature.

Step 2 - Next, fill a pot with water, salt, and oil. After the water is boiled, add you macaroni and cook it.

Step 3 - In a little pan, melt the cannabutter and add the flour. Cook for about five minutes, until everything is smooth and remember to stir it continuously.

Step 4 - Now add the warm milk and then cook it for a few more minutes till the mixture thickens a little.

Step 5 - Add some cheese, salt, paprika, pepper, and nutmeg, and stir them together.

Step 6 - Add the cooked macaroni and mix them well. Pour into small finger bowls.

Step 7 - In a dish, mix the canola oil with the sharp cheddar and some breadcrumbs.

Step 8 - Sprinkle the mixture on top and put in the oven for about 30 minutes until the top becomes brown color. Serve and enjoy!

Chapter 8 - Lemon Canna Dressing Salad with Spaghetti

If you are a vegan, you must know that it could be difficult sometimes to find your favorite Marijuana infused meals readily available in a recipe that meets your diet. Well, if you are reading this, your search is over. Here's a fresh and tasty snack that you will love regardless of whether you are a vegan or not. The greatest of all, it comprises no allergens, just pure plant nutrients, and some ganja. The attendance of THC in this formula is mainly in the dressing, which you could retain for later meals to top salads or vegetable dishes so that you could enjoy this medical help with any other dish too. This formula can serve 3 to 4 people and only takes approximately 1 hour to prepare and cook.

Spaghetti Ingredients:

- One medium to large-sized raw spaghetti squash
- Three tablespoons of drained capers
- A ¼ cup of marinated sundried tomatoes
- ½ thin sliced cucumber
- A ½ cup of chopped fresh parsley

Sauce Ingredients:

- One teaspoon of dijon mustard
- Two tablespoons of white wine vinegar
- ¼ cup of Canna-Oil
- ¼ cup of olive oil
- Two tablespoons of fresh lemon juice
- Sage, Paprika, marjoram, salt, and pepper

Canna-Oil Ingredients:

- 1 to 1 and a ½ ounces of finely ground Cannabis, buds or trim
- Twenty-eight ounces of olive oil

Canna-Oil Instructions:

- First, boil your oil in the saucepan on a low to medium heat. Ensure that it doesn't boil.
- After hot enough, drop in the 1 to 1 and a ½ ounces of excellent ground Marijuana and stir thoroughly.
- The key here is to mix so that the oil doesn't get too hot.

•   After you have been slow cooking the buds for about 1.5 to 2 hours, take them off the cooktop.

•   Drizzle the mixture through a cheesecloth and into the container that you will be keeping your silky Canna-mixture.

•   Put the jar of Canna-Oil in a dark place or the fridge for storage.

Instructions:

Step 1 - First, cut your spaghetti squash in half and remove the seeds.

Step 2 - Put them in a glass baking plate. Rub the cut squash with a little Canna-Oil and add some salt.

Step 3 - Warmth your oven to 400 degrees Fahrenheit or about 200 degrees Celsius and bake the squash for 30 to 45 minutes or till it becomes soft.

Step 4 - Though your squash is baking, make the other vegetables. Chop the parsley and cucumbers and drain the capers and sundried tomatoes.

Step 5 - Blend your dressing by placing all the sauce ingredients in a container and whisking them together.

Step 6 - Finish it by seasoning it; pick any ones you like and add to create some taste.

Step 7 - While the squash is gets cooked, take a fork and pull off strands of the inside, placing all of the pulled pieces in a giant bowl.

Step 8 - After only the squash skin left, you must add in your other components to the large bowl and discard the skin.

Step 9 - Add in the chopped vegetables, sundried tomatoes, and capers. Top off with your delicious Canna-Oil dressing.

Step 10 - Combine the contents of the bowl, then serve and enjoy!

Sandwiches & Burgers

Chapter 9 - Grilled PB & J Herb Sandwich

In case you are looking to cook a classic meal, this is it. In fact, you most likely had it as a child. Perhaps your mom used to make it for you? Either way, today you have a chance to make it yourself by following this simply formula. For this recipe, you are going to want some CannaButter.

CannaButter Instructions:

First of all, the cooking ratio: Utilize approximately 1 cup of butter for each ½ ounce of Cannabis.

1. Start with spreading your ground nuggets, jiggle or trim equally onto a baking sheet with a baking paper. Heat your oven to 240 Degrees Fahrenheit or 115 Degrees Celsius, and bake it for about 40 to 50 minutes. It will turn out very dry, but this is the result you want.

2. In a medium cooking pan, heat 1 or 2 quarts of water and allow this to get hot. After ready, throw in your sticks of butter, but remember; two sticks for ½ ounce grass. Retain the heat on medium-low to slowly melt the butter.

3. Subsequently, the butter has melted; add in those dank buds you just defined in the stove. Mixing it regularly, and allow it to cook on your lowest heat setting for 2½ to 3½ hours.

4. After the dough has slow cooked long enough, take a cheesecloth and place it over a bowl substantial sufficient to hold your batch of butter. Dispense the mixture over the cheesecloth and into the pan cautiously. Next, make sure that you wrap the cheesecloth and give it a squeeze to extract any remaining oil.

5. Allow the mixture to cool for about 45 minutes, and then place it in the fridge to cool a little further. While you put this THC laden concoction in the refrigerator, over time, the top layer

will rise separately from the water, and remember that this is the part when you are going to peel off after it's completely separated. Make sure all extra water is scraped off and store your fresh reefer extract in a jar or air-tight container for future usage.

Ingredients:

- Two teaspoons of butter
- One teaspoon of cannabutter
- Two slices of white or whole wheat bread
- One teaspoon of peanut butter
- Two teaspoons of fruit jelly or cherry jelly

Instructions:

Step 1 - Heat the griddle or skillet to 350 degrees F or 175 degrees C.

Step 2 - Spread the butter on a slice of bread -> remember to do this on both sides, and add a thin layer of Cannabutter. You don't need to give your sandwich too much to create a taste by the way.

Step 3 - Spread the peanut butter on the CannaButter slice of bread, and jelly on the other. Place one slice, buttered side down on the grill. Top with another slice, so that the peanut butter and jelly are in the middle.

Step 4 - Cook it for 3.5 minutes on each side or until it gets golden brown, and heat it properly.

Step 5 - Serve and enjoy!

Chapter 10 - Tampered Mini Burgers

You must know that feeling when you want a juicy burger, right? Yes, I am talking about those that are roofed with cheese and melt while you eat them. Well, if you know what I am suggesting here, you will love this formula — designed to leave you to be energetic any time of the day!

Canna-Oil Ingredients:

•   1-1 ½ ounces of finely ground Cannabis, buds or trim.
•   Twenty-eight ounces of cooking oil, which is always better with olive oil.

Canna-Oil Instructions:

•   First, boil your oil in the saucepan on a low to medium heat. Ensure that it doesn't boil.
•   After hot enough, drop in the 1 to 1 and a ½ ounces of excellent ground Marijuana and stir thoroughly.
•   The key here is to mix so that the oil doesn't get too hot.

- After you have been slow cooking the buds for about 1.5 to 2 hours, take them off the cooktop.
- Drizzle the mixture through a cheesecloth and into the container that you will be keeping your silky Canna-mixture.
- Put the jar of Canna-Oil in a dark place or the fridge for storage.

Marijuana Mini Burgers Ingredients:

- Three small brown onions
- 250g of beef mince
- 1/3 cup of dried breadcrumbs
- One lightly beaten egg
- 1/2 cup of tomato chutney
- 20g of butter
- Two tablespoons of brown sugar
- One tablespoon of balsamic vinegar
- Canna-Oil
- Six hamburger buns
- Cheese Slices
- Sliced Tomatoes and Onion

Instructions:

Step 1 – Start to finely chop about half an onion. Put the following into a bowl; chopped onion, mince, breadcrumbs, egg, and one tablespoon of chutney.

Step 2 - Next, season with salt and pepper and start to mix them together.

Step 3 - After everything is mixed, roll a tablespoons into the mixture to make as big ball as possible.

Step 4 - Squash them slightly to get a hamburger shape and put them in the fridge for about 10 minutes on a platter.

Step 5 - Next, you must spray a large frying pot your Canna-Oil. Warmth over medium-high heat.

Step 6 - Cook 6 patties for 3 to 4 minutes each side or till is cooked through. Ensure you don't overcook them. Medium well is the greatest for this formula by the way.

Step 7 - If you need a slightly higher dose of THC, you could likewise pour a teaspoon of your Canna-Oil into your combination before you start to fry it.

Step 8 - Finally, cut your buns and put the mini burgers inside them. Tribute with a cheese slice and tomatoes. Serve and enjoy!

MEET DISHES

Chapter 11 - THC Fried Chicken

Fried Chicken isn't just delicious, but this formula is guaranteed to leave you craving even more. It is the most delicious, crispiest, the homemade fried chicken you will ever make. This will not only leave you craving for extra, but by adding some killer THC to the equation, it will leave you energetic too anytime of the day. So, if you are ready – let's begin! Ahh! - make sure you have some Canna-Oil ready before get going, but if you are running out, here is how to create some.

Canna-Oil Ingredients:

• 1-1 ½ ounces of finely ground Cannabis, buds or trim.
• Twenty-eight ounces of cooking oil, which is always better with olive oil.

Canna-Oil Instructions:

• First, boil your oil in the saucepan on a low to medium heat. Ensure that it doesn't boil.

- After hot enough, drop in the 1 to 1 and a ½ ounces of excellent ground Marijuana and stir thoroughly.
- The key here is to mix so that the oil doesn't get too hot.
- After you have been slow cooking the buds for about 1.5 to 2 hours, take them off the cooktop.
- Drizzle the mixture through a cheesecloth and into the container that you will be keeping your silky Canna-mixture.
- Put the jar of Canna-Oil in a dark place or the fridge for storage.

Fried Chicken Ingredients:

- 3 cups of all-purpose flour
- 1 and a 1/2 tablespoons of garlic salt
- One tablespoon of ground black pepper
- One tablespoon of paprika
- 1/2 teaspoon of poultry seasoning
- One teaspoon salt
- 1/4 teaspoon ground black pepper
- Two beaten egg yolks
- 1 and a 1/2 cups of beer or water
- 1/2 quart vegetable oil for frying
- 1/2 quart of Canna-Oil
- One whole chicken, cut into pieces

Instructions:

Step 1 - First, you are going to want two separate bowls, as you are going to be mixing different ingredients. In one dish mix 3 cups of flour, garlic, salt, one tablespoon black pepper, paprika, and poultry seasoning.

Step 2 - In the other bowl, mix 1 and a 1/3 cups of flour, salt, 1/4 teaspoon of pepper, egg yolks, and beer. In case the butter came out too thick, utilize some new beer if possible.

Step 3 - Warmth the oil in a fryer to about 350 degrees Fahrenheit. Moisturize each piece of chicken with a little water, at that point dip in the dry mixture.

Step 4 - Shake off the extra and dip in the wet mix, at that point dip in the dry blend after more to get it tender and then to make the mixture stick.

Step 5 - Place the chicken in the oil and Canna-Oil combination, and fry it around 18 minutes or until is browned in color.

Step 6 - After you have removed the chicken from the stove, place on a paper towel to absorb the oil. Serve and enjoy!

Chapter 12 - Homemade Grass Schnitzels

Schnitzels are my husbands all times favourites, and this is why I have been cooking this formula many many time over the past two decades. This is a little time consuming, but here is my version of Homemade Grass Schnitzels. First, you'll want some Canna-Oil.

Canna-Oil Ingredients:

•   1-1 ½ ounces of finely ground Cannabis, buds or trim.
•   Twenty-eight ounces of cooking oil, which is always better with olive oil.

Canna-Oil Instructions:

•   First, boil your oil in the saucepan on a low to medium heat. Ensure that it doesn't boil.
•   After hot enough, drop in the 1 to 1 and a ½ ounces of excellent ground Marijuana and stir thoroughly.
•   The key here is to mix so that the oil doesn't get too hot.

• After you have been slow cooking the buds for about 1.5 to 2 hours, take them off the cooktop.
• Drizzle the mixture through a cheesecloth and into the container that you will be keeping your silky Canna-mixture.
• Put the jar of Canna-Oil in a dark place or the fridge for future usage.

Ingredients:

• Two eggs at least
• Two pounds of skinless and boneless chicken
• One packet of breadcrumbs
• Paprika
• Salt
• Oil for frying

Instructions:

Step 1 - First things first, you'll want to cut up your schnitzels and pound them to a thickness that you favor. My husband prefers small bite-size schnitzels around 1/4 inch thick, but if you or your husband like bigger ones, the principle is the same.

Step 2 - Set up three full shallow bowls first.

Step 3 - Next, in your first bowl, you must beat your eggs, and in the second bowl, you have to stir them together with the paprika, breadcrumbs, and 1 tsp of salt. This is a particular preference, so just remember you could add salt any time later on.

Step 4 - Next, leave an empty plate close where you will put your coated schnitzels.

Step 5 - Pour your oil into your frying pan. The oil could reach a 1/4 height of the schnitzels.

Step 6 - Next, add your tablespoon of Canna-Oil and mix them. Warmth to 375 degrees Farenheight, and fry the coated breasts in single-layer batches till they are golden brown color on both sides. In case your oil is at the right temperature, it could take about 5 minutes for each side.

Step 7 - After frying them, set the schnitzels on a paper towel and pat them dry to soak off excess oil.

Step 8 - Serve and enjoy!

Chapter 13 - Homemade GrassBalls in Tomato Sauce

Not sure about you, but if winter time comes, I love those warm hot dishes that just melt in your mouth☺ Sure, you might go ahead and make the standard meatballs, but if you follow this formula, this is going to be a meal that you will never forget.

Canna-Oil Ingredients:

•   1-1 ½ ounces of finely ground Cannabis, buds or trim.
•   Twenty-eight ounces of cooking oil, which is always better with olive oil.

Canna-Oil Instructions:

•   First, boil your oil in the saucepan on a low to medium heat. Ensure that it doesn't boil.
•   After hot enough, drop in the 1 to 1 and a ½ ounces of excellent ground Marijuana and stir thoroughly.
•   The key here is to mix so that the oil doesn't get too hot.

- After you have been slow cooking the buds for about 1.5 to 2 hours, take them off the cooktop.
- Drizzle the mixture through a cheesecloth and into the container that you will be keeping your silky Canna-mixture.
- Put the jar of Canna-Oil in a dark place or the fridge for storage.

GrassBalls Ingredients:

- 1 pound of lean ground beef
- 1 cup of fresh bread crumbs
- One tablespoon of dried parsley
- One tablespoon of grated Parmesan cheese
- 1/4 teaspoon of ground black pepper
- 1/8 teaspoon of garlic powder
- One egg

Sauce Ingredients:

- 3/4 cup of chopped onion
- Five cloves of minced garlic
- 1/4 cup of olive oil
- 2 cans of whole peeled tomatoes
- Two teaspoons of salt
- One teaspoon of white sugar
- One bay leaf

- One can of tomato paste
- 3/4 teaspoon of dried basil

Instructions:

Step 1 - In a large dish, mix all of the ingredients mentioned above. Mix them well and roll into small balls. Store them in a cool area until desired.

Step 2 - In a big pot over medium temperature, add onion and garlic in the olive oil, and start cooking till the onion is starting glowing.

Step 3 - Next, stir in tomatoes, sugar, salt, and bay leaf. Conceal and decrease the heat to low temperature and simmer for 1 and a half hour.

Step 4 - Finally, stir in the tomato paste, the basil, 1/2 teaspoon of pepper, and meatballs and simmer for about 45 more minutes.

Step 5 - Serve and enjoy!

Chapter 14 - Kush Chicken in a Pot

You must know the feeling when you come home, and you need to chill out and eat something super delicious without putting any energy into it right? Well, this formula is just for those moments. The Kush Chicken in a Pot method will make your buds taste go wild and leave you relaxed in a mellow attitude.

Canna-Oil Ingredients:

•   1-1 ½ ounces of finely ground Cannabis, buds or trim.
•   Twenty-eight ounces of cooking oil, which is always better with olive oil.

Canna-Oil Instructions:

•   First, boil your oil in the saucepan on a low to medium heat. Ensure that it doesn't boil.
•   After hot enough, drop in the 1 to 1 and a ½ ounces of excellent ground Marijuana and stir thoroughly.
•   The key here is to mix so that the oil doesn't get too hot.

- After you have been slow cooking the buds for about 1.5 to 2 hours, take them off the cooktop.
- Drizzle the mixture through a cheesecloth and into the container that you will be keeping your silky Canna-mixture.
- Put the jar of Canna-Oil in a dark place or the fridge for storage.

Ingredients:

- 3/4 cup of chicken broth
- 1 and a 1/2 tablespoons of tomato paste
- 1/4 teaspoon of ground black pepper
- 1/2 teaspoon of dried oregano
- 1/8 teaspoon of salt
- One clove of minced garlic
- Four boneless, skinless chicken breast
- Three tablespoons of dry bread crumbs
- Two teaspoons of olive oil
- 2 cups of fresh sliced mushrooms
- 2 Carrots

Instructions:

Step 1 - In a medium dish, mix the broth, tomato paste, ground black pepper, oregano, salt, and garlic. Blend them all up and put it apart.

Step 2 - Shelter the chicken in bread crumbs, and make sure they are coated well enough.

Step 3 - Next, warm up the oil in a big skillet over medium temperature. Add 1-2 tablespoons of your Canna-Oil.

Step 4 - Next, saute the chicken in the oil for 2 minutes per side, or till they are lightly browned in color.

Step 5 - Add the broth mixture, and your sliced mushrooms and carrots to the skillet and bring them to a boil. At this period you could add a bit more Canna-Oil in case you need to gear it up.

Step 6 - Also, cover it and reduce the heat to low and simmer for 20 minutes.

Step 7 - Eliminate chicken and set aside, and cover to keep it while is still warm.

Step 8 - Lastly, bring the broth mixture to a boil and cook for an additional 4 minutes.

Step 9 - Finally, pour a bit of the sauce over the chicken, and you are ready to go.

Step 10 - Serve and enjoy!

Chapter 15 - Canna Chicken Fajitas

Relish being fried with some delightful chicken fajitas, that only necessitates 30 minutes to cook. This dish is perfect for anyone, and it's loaded up with some active THC and medicinal CBD. For this formula, you will need some Canna-Oil.

Canna-Oil Ingredients:

•   1-1 ½ ounces of finely ground Cannabis, buds or trim.
•   Twenty-eight ounces of cooking oil, which is always better with olive oil.

Canna-Oil Instructions:

•   First, boil your oil in the saucepan on a low to medium heat. Ensure that it doesn't boil.
•   After hot enough, drop in the 1 to 1 and a ½ ounces of excellent ground Marijuana and stir thoroughly.
•   The key here is to mix so that the oil doesn't get too hot.

- After you have been slow cooking the buds for about 1.5 to 2 hours, take them off the cooktop.
- Drizzle the mixture through a cheesecloth and into the container that you will be keeping your silky Canna-mixture.
- Put the jar of Canna-Oil in a dark place or the fridge for storage.

Ingredients:

- A ⅓ cup of Marijuana Oil
- Three chicken breasts boneless & skinless
- One sliced onion
- Two caps of lime juice
- Two bell peppers - sliced
- One teaspoon of chili powder
- One teaspoon of paprika powder
- Salt & black pepper

Instructions:

Step 1 - Begin by pouring your ⅓ cup of Marijuana Oil into a medium to large cast iron pan, and place the oil on a low to medium heat so it can gradually warm up.

Step 2 - After is warm enough, throw your onions and bell peppers onto the pan and allow them to saute slightly.

Step 3 - After your veggies are sauteed, place the chicken breast onto the hot pan and allow this to steam cook. Make sure to flip over the meat with a spatula a few times to get an even coating of the ganja oil on the chicken.

Step 4 - Top off the meat with seasonings; dust the chicken with paprika, chili powder, lime juice, salt and pepper to create some good taste.

Step 5 - Serve and enjoy!

Chapter 16 - Marijuana Chicken Avocado Chili

There is no better dish to add Marijuana to then this California cuisine inspired soup, and this is why you should add this recipe to your after lunch or dinner. This formula is simple, delightful, and will require some medical Canna-Oil.

Canna-Oil Ingredients:

•   1-1 ½ ounces of finely ground Cannabis, buds or trim.
•   Twenty-eight ounces of cooking oil, which is always better with olive oil.

Canna-Oil Instructions:

•   First, boil your oil in the saucepan on a low to medium heat. Ensure that it doesn't boil.
•   After hot enough, drop in the 1 to 1 and a ½ ounces of excellent ground Marijuana and stir thoroughly.
•   The key here is to mix so that the oil doesn't get too hot.

- After you have been slow cooking the buds for about 1.5 to 2 hours, take them off the cooktop.
- Drizzle the mixture through a cheesecloth and into the container that you will be keeping your silky Canna-mixture.
- Put the jar of Canna-Oil in a dark place or the fridge for storage.

After you've got your aromatic oil, you're ready to start cooking. This ground-breaking dish serves six people and only takes about 20 minutes to make.

Ingredients:

- 6 cups of chicken broth
- 4 cups of cooked shredded chicken breast
- A ¾ cup of Marijuana Oil
- 30 ounces of cooked and drained beans
- 4 ounces of cilantro
- Two diced avocados
- Two sprigs of chopped green onion
- Four handfuls of crushed tortilla chips

Instructions:

Step 1 - First, take your chicken broth, shredded chicken, Great Northern Beans, and Marijuana Oil and place them all in a large saucepan.

Step 2 - Begin heating the mixture, frequently stirring to keep a consistent temperature and spread the infusion of Canna-Oil throughout the pot.

Step 3 - After the broth is hot and the shredded chicken is warmed throughout the meat, add in your chopped green onion and cilantro.

Step 4 - Finally, dish up your soup and add in chopped avocado and crushed tortilla chips for added texture and flavour.

Step 5 - Serve, and enjoy!

Chapter 17 - Turkey Sausage Potato Hash

You perhaps know people who distinguish the art of cooking with Cannabis, right?

This is precisely that reason why it's such a great way to start your morning rather cooking and eating some hot Turkey sausage, instead of smoking. – And guess what!? - This Turkey Sausage Potato Hash is the picture-perfect breakfast you can ever imagine.

It serves about 2 to 3 people and done in just 45 minutes. Moreover, you could exchange most of the ingredients with delicious foods that you have lying around in your fridge and create all sorts of variations of this dish.

Ingredients:

*   A ⅛ cup of Marijuana Oil
*   4 cups of diced potatoes
*   One medium-sized sliced onion
*   Two turkey sausages sliced
*   Three large eggs
*   Paprika, Ground sage, cayenne, salt, and pepper

Canna-Oil Ingredients:

- 1-1 ½ ounces of finely ground Cannabis, buds or trim.
- Twenty-eight ounces of cooking oil, which is always better with olive oil.

Canna-Oil Instructions:

- First, boil your oil in the saucepan on a low to medium heat. Ensure that it doesn't boil.
- After hot enough, drop in the 1 to 1 and a ½ ounces of excellent ground Marijuana and stir thoroughly.
- The key here is to mix so that the oil doesn't get too hot.
- After you have been slow cooking the buds for about 1.5 to 2 hours, take them off the cooktop.
- Drizzle the mixture through a cheesecloth and into the container that you will be keeping your silky Canna-mixture.
- Put the jar of Canna-Oil in a dark place or the fridge for storage.

Instructions:

Step 1 - First, in a medium skillet on low heat, warmth about ⅛ cup of Canna-Oil.

Step 2 - Once is hot enough, raise it to medium temperature and add in your 4 cups of diced potatoes.

Step 3 - Next, cook the pieces in the reefer oil for 10 to 15 minutes, and mix them with a spatula.

Step 4 - Complement in the sliced onion and sliced turkey sausage pieces to the skillet. Let them cook an additional 5 to 10 minutes or until the potatoes are beginning to crisp just a little.

Step 5 - Add some paprika, sage, cayenne, pepper, and salt to create some taste, or any spices you wish. Blend the fillings of the skillet with a spatula.

Step 6 - In the last 5 to 10 minutes of cooking, add in your three eggs and let them fry while mixing them slightly with the potatoes and other ingredients.

Step 7 – Serve and enjoy!

Chapter 18 - Dank Baked Pizza

Any 420-friendly folks out there, there is no better arrangement than a freshly made pizza with some Cannabis right? You can either celebrate by yourself or with your Marijuana loving networks this delicious Pizza formula that is not only easy to cook but looks appealing too.

This method is for a Margherita style pizza, yet you could get extra components with your favorite veggies and meats. You could even top this recipe off with a little Keef powder in case that's what you love. First of all, to get the THC content in your tasty treat, make sure that you have some Marijuana Oil lying around. In case you don't have any readily available, here's how to make your own. It does necessitates a little tolerance, but it's a must have.

Dank Canna-Oil Ingredients:

- 1 to 1 ½ ounces of finely ground Cannabis
- 28 ounces of coconut oil or extra virgin olive oil
- A big saucepan
- Stirring spoon
- 1 Cheesecloth

- Airtight vessel to hold the oil

Instructions:

1. First, you have to boil your olive oil or coconut oil in the pot on a low to medium temperature, making sure that it does not boil but gets very hot.

2. After the oil is hot enough, drop in the 1 to 1 ½ ounces of your excellent ground Marijuana and stir thoroughly.

3. Stir frequently but ensure the oil does not begin to boil.

4. After you have been slow cooking the buds for approximately 2 hours, stop the stove.

5. Pour the blend through a cheesecloth and into the vessel that you will be keeping your Canna-mix.

6. Squeeze the cheesecloth to get each last drop of the mixture into the bowl or jar.

7.   Place the pot of Canna-Oil in a dark place or the fridge for storage.

After you have your oil prepared, it's time to get the pizza baking. This formula makes one pizza, depending on the size of your crust, but it can take approximately 35 to 45 minutes to cook.

Ingredients:

- One can of pizza sauce
- ¼-½ cup of Marijuana Oil
- One pizza crust
- One large ripe tomato
- One clove of minced garlic
- Fresh basil
- One pack of Mozzarella cheese

Instructions:

Step 1 - Heat the oven to 400 degrees Fahrenheit or roughly 200 degrees Celsius.

Step 2 - While the oven is warming up, take your can of pizza sauce, the ¼-½ cup

Marijuana Oil and a small pot, and mix the ingredients.

Step 3 - Stir them regularly on a medium heat and get the sauce to a light boil, while allow this sauce to cool on the side.

Step 4 - Next, put your pizza crust on a lightly greased pizza tray, and put it in the oven to bake for a few minutes in case is essential.

Step 5 - Eliminate the coating and spread the freshly cooked Canna-tomato sauce on the pizza and make sure you are equally coating the surface.

Step 6 - Enhance the slices of mozzarella, with tomatoes, and basil to your favourite taste. Top them off with minced garlic and some spices that you like.

Step 7 - Place the pizza in the oven for 15 to 25 minutes, or until you think it's ready.

Step 8 - After the pizza is done, in case you need to get serious, sprinkle a little fragrant Keef powder in the place of parmesan cheese.

Step 9 - Your Baked Pizza is complete, serve and enjoy!

Chapter 19 - Cacciatore Canna-Chicken

This Cacciatore Canna-Chicken is bound to be anyone's favorite. It's stimulated from the original Italian guidelines; however, instead of just having fantastic flavor, it will get you intense too.

With its delicious chicken roast, savory sauce, and high effects, it's a perfect meal for any lunch or dinner occasion. The greatest of all, is that is comprises a high potency of THC that fulfills all of your ganja needs and your food cravings as well.

This is a personal favorite of mine, and I am more than happy to share it — as this plate pairs beautifully with a glass of white or even red wine. Hence, join in this reefer insanity, and turn that red sauce green and get prepared to take your mind on an expedition. To begin with, get ahold of your Canna-Oil.

Canna-Oil Ingredients:

•   1-1 ½ ounces of finely ground Cannabis, buds or trim.

• Twenty-eight ounces of cooking oil, which is always better with olive oil.

Canna-Oil Instructions:

• First, boil your oil in the saucepan on a low to medium heat. Ensure that it doesn't boil.
• After hot enough, drop in the 1 to 1 and a ½ ounces of excellent ground Marijuana and stir thoroughly.
• The key here is to mix so that the oil doesn't get too hot.
• After you have been slow cooking the buds for about 1.5 to 2 hours, take them off the cooktop.
• Drizzle the mixture through a cheesecloth and into the container that you will be keeping your silky Canna-mixture.
• Put the jar of Canna-Oil in a dark place or the fridge for storage.

This formula is enough for four people and takes approximately 30 to 40 minutes to create.

Ingredients:

• One jar of your selection of tomato pasta sauce
• A ½ cup of Canna-Oil

- 1 to 1½ packs of skinned chicken breast
- One package of cremini or button mushrooms
- One medium-sized onion
- Rosemary
- Salt and Pepper

Instructions:

Step 1 - First, take 1 to 2 tablespoons of your distributed Canna-Oil and throw it into a big skillet on low temperature. Allow this oil to heat up for a couple of minutes.

Step 2 - Next, open up your pack of chicken breast and throw the pieces onto the hot skillet.

Step 3 - Chop up an onion and the bag of mushrooms then put the pieces in the skillet with the chicken.

Step 4 - Start to cook the mushrooms, chicken, and onion on medium temperature for 10 to 15 minutes or until it gets golden brown color.

Step 5 - Complement a little salt and pepper to create some good taste, but in the meanwhile you could cover the pan with a lid to retain dampness.

Step 6 - While the chicken and veggies are sweltering, in a small container empty your tomato sauce.

Step 7 - Enhance the rest of your ½ cup of Canna-Oil into the bowl.

Step 8 - Drop in a little subtle chopped rosemary, salt and pepper to create taste.

Step 9 - Next, stir this sauce and let it reach a light boil. After it's hot and ready, place it off to the side.

Step 10 - After the chicken is done cooking, pour the ganja-infused tomato sauce over the chicken in the big skillet and mix with a spatula to get it equally coated with sauce.

Step 11 - Serve and enjoy!

Souses & Salsas

Chapter 20 - Marijuana Cod In Caper Souce

Well, I will be honest here and say that anyone tastes this plate will be left astounded by its nutty flavor, nutritional value, and the high times after their plate is clean. What you'll want for this formula is easy. Make sure to grab your most significant batch of Canna-Oil.

Canna-Oil Ingredients:

- 1-1 ½ ounces of finely ground Cannabis, buds or trim.
- Twenty-eight ounces of cooking oil, which is always better with olive oil.

Canna-Oil Instructions:

- First, boil your oil in the saucepan on a low to medium heat. Ensure that it doesn't boil.
- After hot enough, drop in the 1 to 1 and a ½ ounces of excellent ground Marijuana and stir thoroughly.
- The key here is to mix so that the oil doesn't get too hot.

- After you have been slow cooking the buds for about 1.5 to 2 hours, take them off the cooktop.
- Drizzle the mixture through a cheesecloth and into the container that you will be keeping your silky Canna-mixture.
- Put the jar of Canna-Oil in a dark place or the fridge for storage.

Ingredients For Your Chronic Marijuana Cod Dish:
- 4 (6-ounce) cod fillets
- Three tablespoons of jarred marinated capers
- ½ cup freshly chopped dill
- Freshly squeezed juice of 1 lemon
- Four tablespoons of Canna-Oil
- Salt, black pepper and paprika (to taste)

Instructions:

This formula serves 4 and takes roughly 20 minutes to prepare and cook.

Step 1 - First off all, season your fresh cod fillets with salt, black pepper and paprika to create some good taste. Pre-seasoning allows the flavor to soak in during the cooking process.

Step 2 - Get a big skillet and turn on your stovetop to medium temperature. Put one tablespoon of your Canna-Oil in the pan to coat the fillets in Cannabis while they're cooking.

Step 3 - Next, throw your cod fillets on your hot oiled skillet, and allow each side to cook. This process does not take long, in fact is roughly 4 minutes per side. You need the cod to remain soft and buttery, to preserve the texture and melted nature of the fish.

Step 4 - After the fish has cooked, set it aside on a plate.

Step 5 - Within the same pot, add in your capers, fresh chopped dill set aside a little fresh dill for garnish and three extra tablespoons of Canna-Oil. Let the natural juice out, while cooking the cod to blend with your new added components.

Step 6 - Allow these ingredients to all heat up a bit and frequently, yet you must stir with your spatula. Only cook for approximately 5 minutes.

Step 7 - After your sauce is complete, pour it over your cooked cod fillets that you set aside and garnish with your fresh lemon juice and a little fresh dill.

Chapter 21 - Mango Cannabis Salsa

If you adore Mexican cuisine and perhaps searching for the picture-perfect fresh meal that you want to fulfill the Marijuana love in you, then this unbelievable Mango Cannabis Salsa is just the way to go.

Ready with high quality ingredients, plus THC and medicine rich Canna-Oil, Mango Cannabis Salsa has everything you want for a enduring rebound. Start by preparing your Canna-Oil. You could either make it by yourself or buy it from a shop, but in case you already happen to have some around then feel free to bounce this step.

Canna-Oil Ingredients:

•   1-1 ½ ounces of finely ground Cannabis, buds or trim.
•   Twenty-eight ounces of cooking oil, which is always better with olive oil.

Canna-Oil Instructions:

•   First, boil your oil in the saucepan on a low to medium heat. Ensure that it doesn't boil.

- After hot enough, drop in the 1 to 1 and a ½ ounces of excellent ground Marijuana and stir thoroughly.
- The key here is to mix so that the oil doesn't get too hot.
- After you have been slow cooking the buds for about 1.5 to 2 hours, take them off the cooktop.
- Drizzle the mixture through a cheesecloth and into the container that you will be keeping your silky Canna-mixture.
- Put the jar of Canna-Oil in a dark place or the fridge for storage.

Mango Cannabis Salsa Ingredients:

- 2 cups of diced aroma or heirloom tomatoes
- A ½ cup of diced fresh mango
- Four tablespoons of Canna-Oil
- A ¼ cup of fresh chopped cilantro
- One lime squeezed for juice
- ½ cup of red onion or shallot
- Paprika
- Chile powder
- Black pepper
- Salt
- Crushed red pepper
- Any other spices you might desire

Instructions:

Step 1 - First, throw all of your elements into a medium to large serving dish.

Step 2 - Mix all the parts to ensure the Canna-Oil is distributed evenly throughout the meal.

Step 3 - Refrigerate it immediately right after the preparation.

Step 4 - After your Mango Cannabis Salsa has cooled down, serve, and enjoy!

Chapter 22 - Gange Guacamole

Here is another great Mexican dish that will allow you to fiesta into the night. This is the perfect dip for all your upcoming beach days and summer parties.

Ganga Guacamole Ingredients:

- 4 Tsp of Canna-coconut Oil
- 3 Avocados
- 1 Small Red Onion
- 1 Jalapeno
- 1 Red Pepper
- One tbs of lemon juice
- Cilantro
- Salt and Pepper

Preparing the Canna-Coconut Oil

Ingredients:

- Crockpot
- 5 cups of distilled water
- 2 ounces of finely ground Marijuana

- 1 cup of organic coconut oil
- Strainer or cheesecloth
- Tupperware container with lid
- Rubberband

Instructions:

Step 1 - First, you should melt 1 cup of organic coconut oil in the crockpot on the lowest setting.

Step 2 - Add 2 ounces of Marijuana and 5 cups of water while the coconut oil is melting. Mix everything.

Step 3 - Turn the crock pot on high temperature for one hour, and keep on stirring frequently.

Step 4 - Return the crock pot to a low setting. Let the blend to steep for 4 to 24 hours and stir it in each hour.

Step 5 - Turn the crockpot off. Pour the Coconut Marijuana Oil mix little-by-little slowly over the top of the cheesecloth and into the container.

Step 6 - Replicate this step as necessary to strain all of the liquid from the plant.

Step 7 - Conceal the pot and put in the fridge. Postpone overnight for the mixture to separate.

Step 8 - Eliminate the hardened coconut oil from the top and remove the water.

Step 9 - Utilize the Coconut Marijuana Oil in solid form or meltdown as a liquid.

Guacamole Sauce Instructions:

Step 1 - First, cut your avocados in half, and take out the pits. Slice them vertically, then parallel to make little diced pieces of avocado.

Step 2 - Next, spoon out into a bowl, and mash with a fork.

Step 3 - Complement in your 4 tsp of canna-coconut oil, and a tablespoon of lemon or lime juice, whichever you favor.

Step 4 - Blend and mash your avocado with the oil and juice until it's smooth.

Step 5 - Dice up your onion, pepper, and jalapeno and then mix into your guac.

Step 6 - Add salt, pepper, and cilantro to create some good taste.

Step 7 - Lastly, smear it all over your favorite Mexican plates, go at it with a spoon, or else dip your chips in this delicious Guacamole.

Step 8 - Serve and enjoy!

FISH MEALS

Chapter 23 - Tuna Salad with Cannabis

Just imagine that you are going to host a lunch party or barbeque that 420 friendly guests will be showing up right? Well, if it's about to happen, you might go ahead and try out this Tuna Salad with Cannabis, which could be jkust the perfect formula for you. For this method, you'll want a fresh batch of Canna-Oil.

Canna-Oil Ingredients:

• 1-1 ½ ounces of finely ground Cannabis, buds or trim.
• Twenty-eight ounces of cooking oil, which is always better with olive oil.

Canna-Oil Instructions:

• First, boil your oil in the saucepan on a low to medium heat. Ensure that it doesn't boil.
• After hot enough, drop in the 1 to 1 and a ½ ounces of excellent ground Marijuana and stir thoroughly.
• The key here is to mix so that the oil doesn't get too hot.

- After you have been slow cooking the buds for about 1.5 to 2 hours, take them off the cooktop.
- Drizzle the mixture through a cheesecloth and into the container that you will be keeping your silky Canna-mixture.
- Put the jar of Canna-Oil in a dark place or the fridge for storage.

Ingredients:

- A ¼ cup of Canna-Oil
- 12 ounces of drained tuna
- Four tablespoons of mayonnaise
- Two green onions chopped
- Two stalks of chopped celery
- Paprika, salt & black pepper, and sage

This formula serves four people and takes about 1 hour and 25 minutes to make.

Instructions:

Step 1 - First, grab a big mixing bowl and combine the tuna, green onions, and celery.

Step 2 - Cover the mixture with four tablespoons of mayonnaise and then pour over your ¼ cup of Canna-Oil.

Step 3 - Blend all the components carefully in the dish, and then top off with your favorite seasonings to create some taste.

Step 4 - Put the container of Chronic Tuna Salad in the refrigerator to cool for about 1 hour.

Step 5 - After the mixture has chilled, serve and enjoy!

Chapter 24 - Medical Pasta with Shrimp & Spinach

Perhaps you don't want to devote a lot of time cooking dinner but still need to feel the medical relief of Cannabis? If your answer is yes, this is just the recipe for you.

Preparing your medical pasta takes a very little time, as long as you have some of your precious Cannabutter laying around.

After your butter is ready to go, this recipe requires just a few ingredients, and only has a cook time of 20 minutes, and serves four people.

Ingredients:

- A ¾ pound of short style pasta
- Four tablespoons of your Cannabutter
- Two leeks diced
- 1 pound of cleaned shrimp
- 7 ounces of baby spinach
- Five tablespoons of sundried tomatoes
- Salt and pepper
- Three tablespoons of olive oil
- Grated lemon zest

CannaButter Instructions:

First of all, the cooking ratio: Utilize approximately 1 cup of butter for each ½ ounce of Cannabis.

1. Start with spreading your ground nuggets, jiggle or trim equally onto a baking sheet with a baking paper. Heat your oven to 240 Degrees Fahrenheit or 115 Degrees Celsius, and bake it for about 40 to 50 minutes. It will turn out very dry, but this is the result you want.

2. In a medium cooking pan, heat 1-2 quarts of water and allow this to get hot. After ready, throw in your sticks of butter, but remember; two sticks for ½ ounce grass. Retain the heat on medium-low to slowly melt the butter.

3. Subsequently, the butter has melted; add in those dank buds you just defined in the stove. Mixing it regularly, and allow it to cook on your lowest heat setting for 2½ to 3½ hours.

4. After the dough has slow cooked long enough, take a cheesecloth and place it over a bowl substantial sufficient to hold your batch of butter. Dispense the mixture over the cheesecloth and into the pan cautiously. Next, make sure that you wrap the cheesecloth and give it a squeeze to extract any remaining oil.

5. Allow the mixture to cool for about 45 minutes, and then place it in the fridge to cool a little further. While you put this THC laden concoction in the refrigerator, over time, the top layer will rise separately from the water, and remember that this is the part when you are going to peel off after it's completely separated. Make sure all extra water is scraped off and store your fresh reefer extract in a jar or air-tight container for future usage.

Instructions:

Step 1 - In a medium saucepan, boil a little water. Complement with a bit of olive oil and salt.

Step 2 - After the water is boiled, pour it on the top of the pasta and stir periodically.

Step 3 - Cook the pasta for roughly 10 minutes, or till it becomes soft.

Step 4 - While the pasta is getting boiled, in a medium skillet add in your four tablespoons of Cannabutter on low heat.

Step 5 - After the pot has become a little hot, add in your shrimp and chopped leeks.

Step 6 - Turn up to medium temperature. Enhance salt, pepper, lemon zest, and any other spices to create some great taste.

Step 7 - Blend regularly so that the shrimp becomes equally coated with the Cannabutter.

Step 8 - Enhance the spinach at the very end of the cooking process for the shrimp, letting the spinach to wilt just a little bit.

Step 9 - After the pasta is done boiling, drain it with a strainer, place it in a large serving bowl.

Step 10 - After the shrimp has finished cooking, add the mixture into the serving bowl with the pasta.

Step 11 - Complement in your sundried tomatoes, the rest of your olive oil, and more spices to create a great taste.

Step 12 - Lastly, blend your dish carefully, serve, and enjoy!

Chapter 25 - Cannabis Salmon

Not everyone likes fish, but those who do – must know that salmon is one of the best and most delicious fish that is easily accessible and super easy to prepare. Now visualize taking that salmon and diffusing it with some excellent Cannabis. What you get, is a delightful meal that will stay with you for hours. To get going, you're going to want some CannaButter.

CannaButter Instructions:

1. Start with spreading your ground nuggets, jiggle or trim equally onto a baking sheet with a baking paper. Heat your oven to 240 Degrees Fahrenheit or 115 Degrees Celsius, and bake it for about 40 to 50 minutes. It will turn out very dry, but this is the result you want.

2. In a medium cooking pan, heat 1-2 quarts of water and allow this to get hot. After ready, throw in your sticks of butter, but remember; two sticks for ½ ounce grass. Retain the heat on medium-low to slowly melt the butter.

3. Subsequently, the butter has melted; add in those dank buds you just defined in the stove. Mixing it regularly, and allow it to cook on your lowest heat setting for 2½ to 3½ hours.

4. After the dough has slow cooked long enough, take a cheesecloth and place it over a bowl substantial sufficient to hold your batch of butter. Dispense the mixture over the cheesecloth and into the pan cautiously. Next, make sure that you wrap the cheesecloth and give it a squeeze to extract any remaining oil.

5. Allow the mixture to cool for about 45 minutes, and then place it in the fridge to cool a little further. While you put this THC laden concoction in the refrigerator, over time, the top layer will rise separately from the water, and remember that this is the part when you are going to peel off after it's completely separated. Make sure all

extra water is scraped off and store your fresh reefer extract in a jar or air-tight container for future usage.

Ingredients:

- One tablespoon of garlic powder
- One tablespoon of dried basil
- 1/2 teaspoon of salt
- Four salmon
- One tablespoon of butter
- One tablespoon of Cannabutter
- Four lemon wedges

Instructions:

Step 1 - First, stir together the basil, garlic powder, and salt in a small dish, and smear onto the salmon fillets.

Step 2 - Next, melt the butter and Cannabutter together in a skillet over medium temperature; then cook the salmon in the butter till browned and peeling, for about five more minutes each side.

Step 3 - Serve and enjoy!

Vegetarian Dishes

Chapter 26 - Veggie Mari-Lasagna

There are bad days when it is easy to devastate a standard plate with extra elements. Nevertheless, Marijuana oil only makes the veggie lasagna more delicious. To start with the obvious statement, Marijuana oil has been hyped to comprise many things that help the body, and this formula does not only guarantee a sincere mealtime but rich in vital vitamins and natural resources too. Bombshell your friends or family members with your new gastronomic conception with his delicious meal any time of the day.

Ingredients:

- 2 ounces of finely ground Cannabis
- 30 ounces of extra virgin olive oil
- Five tablespoons of flour
- About a quarter gallon of milk
- Nutmeg, salt, pepper, and grated garlic
- Two boxes of lasagna noodles
- One huge carrot
- One big red pepper
- Four tomatoes
- A can of olives

- About 1.5 pounds of mixed cheese (mozzarella, parmesan, Maasdam)
- About 1.5 pounds of Portobello mushrooms

Marijuana oil Instructions:

Step 1 - First, pour the olive oil into the pot and heat it, but circumvent boiling it.

Step 2 - Put the ground Marijuana into the oil and stir it carefully.

Step 3 - Simmer the oil for about 2 hours.

Step 4 - Next, put the oil over a cheesecloth.

Step 5 - Pour it into a dish and close it tightly.

Step 6 - Keep the oil in the cold dark place, preferably the refrigerator.

Bechamel sauce Instructions:

It's hard to make a mistake while you are cooking bechamel sauce, yet it is still possible. Anyhow, your main goal is to avoid lumps.

Step 1 - Take a heavy-bottomed saucepan and pour the Marijuana oil into it.

Step 2 - Heat the pan but don't allow the oil to boil.

Step 3 - Slowly put the flour into the pot and stir energetically.

Step 4 - Remain stirring till the flour gets golden in color.

Step 5 - Next, gradually pour in the milk and stir without stopping till the blend begins boiling.

Step 6 - Add salt and pepper and two teaspoons of nutmeg, and keep stirring.

Step 7 - Boil the sauce for about 5 to 7 minutes while stirring it carefully.

Step 8 - The bechamel sauce shouldn't have any lumps, thus retain stirring until the combination is standardized.

Step 9 - Finally, all the components are prepared, so you can start cooking the lasagna.

After making the Marijuana oil and bechamel sauce, the next task is to develop the lasagna.

Lasagna Instructions:

Step 1 - First, cut the Portobello mushrooms into small bits, place them in a frying pot, and turn the heat up, while you add some salt.

Step 2 - Next, fry the mushrooms till all water evaporates and 5 minutes afterward, start stirring the mixture.

Step 3 - Switch off the heat and leave the mushrooms on a hot frying pot, allowing them to dry out even more.

Step 4 - Though the mushrooms are resting, grate the carrot into large pieces and cut the red pepper into cubes or slices.

Step 5 - Place the mushrooms on a plate to free up the frying pan

Step 6 - Use the high heat, red pepper, fry carrots, black pepper, grated garlic and additional herbs in olive oil for about 5 to 10 seconds.

Step 7 - Next, enhance with a little water, half a teaspoon of salt and steam the ingredients for additional 5 to 7 minutes without covering the pan.

Step 8 - In the meantime, you could slice the tomatoes and olives and grate all the cheeses distinctly.

Step 9 - Take a deep baking bowl and grease it with olive oil.

Step 10 - Using a pass attempt brush or spoon, smear the Bechamel sauce over the whole dish space.

Step 11 - Conceal the bottom with lasagna noodles.

Step 12 - Shelter the noodles with 2/3 of the steamed vegetables.

Step 13 - Pour bechamel sauce on top of it.

Step 14 - Place the parmesan cheese consistently on top of the sauce.

Step 15 - Place the lasagna noodles on top of the cheese.

Step 16 - Place 2/3 of the mushrooms on top of the noodles.

Step 17 - Next, sprinkle the mushrooms with the rest of the parmesan cheese.

Step 18 - Shelter the cheese with more lasagna noodles.

Step 19 - Pour in the béchamel sauce.

Step 20 - Shelter the sauce with the olives and the rest of the mushrooms.

Step 21 - Cover the olives with half Maasdam cheese.

Step 22 - Put the lasagna noodles on top.

Step 22 - Pour sufficiently the bechamel sauce and the mozzarella cheese.

Step 23 - Shelter this layer with more lasagna noodles and pour in some more bechamel sauce.

Step 24 - Place the tomatoes on the top, and add the rest of the vegetables and sprinkle more cheese on the top.

Step 25 - Finally, heat the oven to 375 Fahrenheit and bake the lasagna for roughly 1 hour long.

Step 26 - Serve and enjoy!

Chapter 27 - Veggie Canna Burger with Black Beans

Have you ever experienced that you are about to throw up a party to your Cannabis loving friends, yet the guestlists include vegetarians and you not sure what to prepare for them? Or perhaps you love burgers, but you are a vegetarian and want to cook something that you can mix with some Cannabis? Well, if your answer is yes, you are going to love this Veggie CannaBurger formula. First of all, make sure you have some Canna-Oil ready;

Canna-Oil Ingredients:

• 1-1 ½ ounces of finely ground Cannabis, buds or trim.
• Twenty-eight ounces of cooking oil, which is always better with olive oil.

Canna-Oil Instructions:

• First, boil your oil in the saucepan on a low to medium heat. Ensure that it doesn't boil.

- After hot enough, drop in the 1 to 1 and a ½ ounces of excellent ground Marijuana and stir thoroughly.
- The key here is to mix so that the oil doesn't get too hot.
- After you have been slow cooking the buds for about 1.5 to 2 hours, take them off the cooktop.
- Drizzle the mixture through a cheesecloth and into the container that you will be keeping your silky Canna-mixture.
- Put the jar of Canna-Oil in a dark place or the fridge for storage.

Ingredients:

- A can of drained black beans
- 1/2 green bell pepper - cut into 2-inch pieces
- 1/2 onion - cut into wedges
- Three cloves peeled garlic
- One egg
- One tablespoon of chili powder
- One tablespoon of cumin
- One teaspoon of Thai chili sauce or hot sauce
- 1/2 cup of bread crumbs

Instructions:

Step 1 - Heat the oven to 375 degrees Fahrenheit or 190 degrees Celsius, and carelessly oil a baking sheet.

Step 2 - In a dish, start to mash black beans with a fork until you get a pasty texture. Add a teaspoon of your Canna-Oil and mix them.

Step 3 - You could do this by hand, but a food processor will help. Finely chop your bell pepper, onion, and garlic, and mix with the mashed beans.

Step 4 - In a small dish, stir them together with the chili powder, egg, chili sauce, and cumin.

Step 5 - Next, stir the egg mixture into the mashed beans. Throw in the bread crumbs and stir until the dough is sticky and holds together.

Step 6 - Split the mixture into the size of the burgers you want.

Step 7 - Lastly, put the patties on a baking sheet, and then bake it about 10 minutes on each side, but you could likewise grill these too, if you wish to.

Step 8 - Serve and enjoy!

BOOK 3

23 Delightful Cannabis Candy and Dessert

BY
MARIE SPILOTRO

Chapter 1 – Marijuana-infused Nutella

In each great edibles list, there needs to be a chocolate number for those with the ultimate sweet tooth so that I could think of no better formula for you than this Marijuana infused Nutella. We going to mix it with some nuts, grass, and the most loved chocolate spread, all turned into one awesome method.

Supply Requirements:

- Marijuana-infused oil
- One jar of Nutella
- Mixing bowl

Instructions:

- This is a super quick and simple recipe, so after you have your Nutella and have prepped your Marijuana oil, let's go.
- Put your Nutella into a mixing dish; the quantity is completely up to you, subject to how much you need to put together really.
- For each portion of Nutella, what you you need to do, is mix in with one dose of Marijuana oil. After combined together, stir well until the

oil has been evenly distributed through the chocolate and the oil is no longer visible.

• Keep stored in the fridge, and after it's cold, serve it and enjoy!

Chapter 2 – Grass in Ice Cream

Who doesn't love decent ice cream right? Possibly the single most famous dessert ever, and there is only one thing that could ever make it better: Marijuana! This grass in ice cream makes for the perfect sweet and is pretty stress-free to make it too.

Supply Requirements:

• 500 ml of ice cream – any flavour will do, but you might go with your favourite taste
• 75 g of sugar
• 50 g of Marijuana butter
• 2x Saucepan
• Mixing bowl

Instructions:

• Take the ice cream and heat it in a pan over medium heat, bringing it to a simmer.
• Using your other pot, melt 50 g of Marijuana butter, adding in the sugar to melt together, making a sweet and Marijuana-rich liquid.

- Optional - To group your flavor, mash up the fruit of your choice in a mixing bowl. I personally love strawberries, but you could do any fruit if you like.
- After the fruits are mashed to your anticipated texture, mix all the components, and add to a big bowl.
- Pop your combination into the freezer for a small number of hours until it's frozen, and enjoy!

Chapter 3 - Stoned Gummy Bears

Both; adults as well children do enjoy gummy bear sweets for as long as I can think of, however for the health cognisant these extravagances aren't something I can spoil in regularly, and this formula is only for adults. Enter these half-healthy gummy bears, saturated with Marijuana.

Supply Requirements:

- 2/3 cup of pureed fruit, but I suggest you use berries such as raspberries, blackberries, or even strawberries. Nonetheless, any berry will do the job.
- 1/3 cup of water
- One tablespoon of lemon juice
- Two tablespoons of honey or maple syrup
- 2 to 3 tablespoons of Marijuana tincture
- Three tablespoons of grass-fed gelatin
- A gummy bear
- A saucepan

Instructions:

- Mix your fresh fruit into a pot with 1/3-cup water, sweetener, lemon juice, and put on medium to low heat.
- Add to this mixture your Marijuana solution, and slowly whisk in the grass-fed gelatine.
- Carry on whipping the mixture till smooth and well joined.
- Next, turn off the heat, and using a dropper or spoon, fill your mold with the mixture.
- After about 5 minutes in the freezer, or 15 minutes in the fridge, your bears are all set to be removed from the mold and ready to serve.

Chapter 4 - Flying Bananas

These delightful chocolate-coated bananas are not only quick and straightforward to create; but on the other hand, they taste astonishing and integrate my cannabutter recipe to bring you a lovely little tinkle with each naughty bite!

Supply Requirements:

- Half of a sliced banana
- ½ teaspoon of Marijuana Cannabutter or oil
- One tablespoon of chocolate chips, which can be either white or dark
- Heat-proof bowl
- Parchment paper

Instructions:

- Place your chocolate chips and cannabutter or Marijuana oil into a heatproof bowl that can be placed in the oven.
- Heat slowly over low temperature, allowing the mixture to gently melt without burning or ruining the cannabinoids in the oil - approximately 120 degrees.

- Once it's liquid, stir it till it is smooth with no bumps or lumps.
- Add into the chocolate your bananas - ensuring they are all well coated .
- After you are happy with your bananas, place them on a parchment paper lined baking tray and pop them into the freezer.
- Once it is frozen, you are ready to spoil in your Marijuana pervaded delights.

Chapter 5 - Marijuana Chocolate

There are countless different ways to combine Marijuana and chocolate. Hash brownies are an all-time classic, and Cannabis-infused hot chocolate is the perfect way to warm up on icy winter days.

However, in case you are after a recipe which is quick, easy, and fun to make, this is the one for you.

You only want absolute basic, store cupboard ingredients, and equipment to make this Marijuana-infused chocolate at home. Likewise, it necessitates a minimal amount of talent.

Supply Requirements:

- 3 to 5 gram of high-quality bud
- One parchment paper for decarboxylation and a baking sheet
- 100 gram of dark chocolate, or at least 70% cocoa, and break them into small bits
- Glass container
- One saucepan
- Chocolate mold or an ice cube tray

Instructions:

Step 1: You must decarboxylate your Marijuana
Before you start making your grass-infused chocolate, you want to decarboxylate your bud. This process converts the THCA and CBDA located in raw Cannabis into their more active shapes, CBD and THC. It might seem like an excessive amount of sweat, however decarboxylating your Marijuana is worth doing. In case you skip this and throw fresh grass into your chocolate, you will most likely be disappointed with the results. The easiest way to decarboxylating your grass is to grind it excellently and binge it on parchment paper on a baking sheet. Put the ground bud into an oven which has been preheated to around 240°F or 115°C and bake it for approximately 30 minutes. Check your grass and heat for a further 5 to 10 minutes in case is necessary. While it is ready, it will be dried out and slightly toasted in color, but not burnt. After the decarboxylation process is complete, set your grass on the side, and move onto the next step.

Step 2: Melt Your Chocolate
Locate a bowl which fits at ease into the top of your pot without touching the bottom. Dispense sufficient hot water into your pan to cover the base adequately, but confirm it does not seem to extend as high as the base of the bowl. Put your

broken chocolate into the bowl, then set it over the pot. Put on a medium heat so that the water is simmering but not boiling too hard — this double-boiler technique of cooking guarantees that the chocolate will melt without sticking or burning to the dish. Hold onto stirring your chocolate regularly till it melts into a thick, smooth liquid which is free from bumps, and remove from the heat.

Step 3: Mix in Your Ground Marijuana
Add your ground Marijuana to the chocolate and stir well to ensure that it is distributed evenly. This will work better in case your Marijuana is very finely ground.

Step 4: Pour into Molds
You could purchase individual chocolate molds, or utilize a regular ice cube tray. In a nip, you might even create one large block of chocolate and cut it into squares later on, even though this will be more problematic after your Marijuana chocolate sets firm.

Step 5: Remove the Air Bubbles
Moderately drop your filled molds onto the kitchen counter several times to let air bubbles that are stuck in the chocolate mix. Circumvent overfilling your molds in step 4, so they do not spill.

Step 6: Chill Your Marijuana Chocolate
Place your Marijuana chocolate in the refrigerator to a fix. This might take as little as 10 to 15 minutes but could take longer depending on what type of chocolate you utilize, and how deep your molds are.

Step 7: Enjoy Responsibly!
After your Marijuana chocolate is set, remove it from the molds and enjoy. In case you are new to Cannabis edibles, be advised, they pack a blow. One of these chocolates could be plentiful; therefore, go slow! Edibles equally take up to two hours to kick in, so don't be misled into thinking they aren't functioning and taking an additional dose too quickly.

Additional Notes and Tips:

There are numerous different ways to make Marijuana chocolate, and the above recipe is one of the simplest out there. To get the maximum out of this basic formula, attempt the following tips:

Make use of the Utmost Chocolate you can pay for!

Using high-quality chocolate can elevate your Cannabis edibles to the next level with the minimum amount of effort. The most exceptional chocolate could only include a few ingredients:

Cocoa mass, sugar, and cocoa butter or lecithin. It is likewise a decent idea to utilize the highest cocoa percentage you can find to maximize the potential aids of your chocolate. In case you find dark chocolate overly bitter, you could use white chocolate or milk instead. Conversely, these choices are far less healthy, and in my experience, much less satisfying.

Restrain your Chocolate for a Specialized Look

While moderating your chocolate it isn't 100% necessary, but it does advance the texture of the finished product. Likewise, it decreases the likelihood of your chocolate blooming, implying that it sets with a matt finish and unappealing white spots.

To moderate your chocolate like an expert, you will want a food thermostat. Next, you must melt around two-thirds of your chocolate, and take away from the heat. Add the outstanding chocolate, and return to the heat along with your thermostat. While the temperature reaches 88 to 90°F or 31 to 32°C and the second batch of chocolate has melted, it is tempered and ready for use.

Tempering works well with large quantities of chocolate, and a minimum of 1 kg is advised. Every leftover moderated chocolate can be put away for future use, if it lasts, of course. While you've got the hang of this basic Marijuana chocolate formula, you could mix it up by adding extras such as raisins, nuts, orange zest, popping candy, or even a pinch of chili powder.

You can go ahead and try to experiment with different textures and flavors to find the perfect blend for you.

Chapter 6 - Zonked Kief-Cookie

This is a brilliant formula for those who are entirely new to cooking with Marijuana. Easy to follow, so take your favorite cookie technique and follow these simple steps to get the coolest THC jam-packed cookies – on a realistic price tag. Do not let those little bits of leftover kief go to discarded; in case you don't smoke them; this is the perfect alternative for a zero-waste lifestyle that will pack one hell of a punch.

Supply Requirements:

• For this formula, you want to utilize your standard cookie ingredients
• An oven
• Leftover kief

Instructions:

• As I mentioned, this formula is super simple and easy to follow, especially in case you've not ever cooked edibles previously!
• Using your favorite cookie recipe, get your kief together while the oven warms up.

- Heat your kief in the oven for a small number of minutes before the kief is ready to go in.
- After prepared, sprinkle your kief onto the cookie dough before putting it into the oven.
- It is as simple as that.
- Remember that kief is a flower, and therefore considerably more robust, so bear this in mind while spoiling!

Chapter 7 – Cannabis-Cupcakes

Who doesn't love a cupcake right? You don't have to be below the age of 10 to enjoy an icing-topped cake, particularly one that freshly out the oven, baked with your premium Marijuana right? This formula takes a little more experience, nevertheless it is still pretty straightforward and is super delightful, and of course, you will get high!

Supply Requirements:

- ¼ Milk and ¼ Yogurt
- 1 Tablespoon of hemp oil
- ¼ Cup of Agave
- A Teaspoon of Vanilla extract
- ¾ Cup of all-purpose flour
- ¼ Baking soda
- Salt
- 1 Tablespoon of cornstarch
- 1 Teaspoon of baking powder
- ¼ Teaspoon of baking powder

Supply requirements for the Frosting:

- 2 Tablespoons of cannabutter

- A Teaspoon of vanilla extract
- 2 Tablespoons of strawberry jam
- 2 ½ Cups of sugar

Instructions:

- It is a pretty laid-back recipe to follow that starts with turning on the oven on and preheat it to about 330 to 350 degrees.
- In a medium to large size bowl, whisk together the yogurt and vanilla extract.
- After mixed, go through all the dry elements into the wet; and confirm they are combined properly.
- Line a cupcake pot with liners and fill every two thirds full with the mixture, pop into the oven then bake it for 20 to 25 minutes. In case unsure, apply a cake tester and ensure that it comes out completely clean, meaning the cakes are cooked inside.
- For the frosting, mix the butter and sugar on low speed, then add in the strawberry jam a spoonful at a time.
- Finally, add in the vanilla and utilize a piping bag to garnish your cakes while cooled.
- Serve and enjoy!

Chapter 8 – Cannab-Ice-Cream

Ice cream is an everlasting classic of a dessert, which is always nice to have in the freezer, ready to be consumed right? This formula is customizable, and you could decide for whatever ingredients you like to flavor it to your preference.

Supply Requirements:

- 500ml of Double cream
- 50g of Marijuana butter
- 75g of Sugar
- Fruit of your choice, I love strawberries, bananas, and blueberries☺

Instructions:

- This super simple formula, start by adding in a large pan the double cream first.
- Next, heat it over to a medium temperature until it begins to rumble.
- In a separate pan, melt about 50 grams of cannabutter and 75 grams of sugar together, and mix them well.

- Mashup your fruit of choice in a separate container till you are happy with the steadiness.
- Add all the ingredients into a large bowl and pop into the freezer overnight.
- Like I said; simple and easy, right? Enjoy!

Chapter 9 - Cannasmoothie

Everyone loves a fruity and refreshing smoothie with a bit of a nutrient kick right? In case you are craving a boost, why not give this tasty canna-smoothie a go? All the help of a fruit smoothie, but with a twist!

Supply Requirements:

- Two tablespoons of canna-coconut oil
- One frozen banana, sliced
- 1 to 2 cups of coconut milk
- 2 cups of frozen strawberries
- Four tablespoons of pomegranate juice
- Two tablespoons of pomegranate molasses for drizzling
- Small skillet

Instructions:

1. First, heat your homemade canna-coconut oil in a small skillet. After hot, add in your sliced banana and allow this to cook for 3 to 4 minutes, stirring occasionally.

2. Next, take this off the heat and allow it calm.

3. In the time being, place the rest of your ingredients, excluding the molasses, into a blender.

4. Next, add in your now cooled down banana in the cannabutter and blitz the entire mixture until all smooth.

5. Distribute between two glasses, sprinkle on the pomegranate molasses, and enjoy!

Chapter 10 - Grass Carrot Cake

I will be frank here and say that this is a creepy one and might not be for everybody, but before you move to the next recipe, let me tell you that I was surprised at this formula. It was very appealing, and as a result, here it is my variety of Homemade Delicious Grass Carrot Cake. To get started with this one, you'll want a little Canna Oil.

Marijuana Oil with Basic Ingredients:

*   1 to 1 ½ ounces of finely ground Cannabis, buds or trim
*   28 ounces of cooking oil, and for that, follow the instructions below

How to make your Canna Oil:

*   First, boil your oil in the pot on a low to medium heat. Ensure that it doesn't burn.
*   After is hot enough, drop in the 1 to 1 ½ ounces of your outstanding Marijuana and stir.
*   Stir, so the Marijuana doesn't burn.

- After you have been slow cooking the buds for roughly 1.5 to 2 hours, take them off the cooktop.
- Pour the combination through a cheesecloth and into a jar that you will be keeping your mixture.
- Place the pot of Canna Oil in a dark place or the fridge for storage

Grass Carrot Cake Ingredients:

- 175g of light sugar
- 175ml of sunflower oil
- 40ml of Canna oil
- Three large eggs, and make sure they are lightly beaten
- 140 g of grated carrot
- 100 gram of raisins
- Grated zest of 1 large orange
- 175g of self-raising flour
- 1 tsp of bicarbonate soda
- 1 tsp of ground of cinnamon
- ½ tsp of grated nutmeg, if you use freshly grated one, it will give you the most significant flavor

Instructions:

Step 1 - First, you must make sure that you pre-heat the oven to 180 Celsius, and then line and oil the base and sides of an 18 cm of square baking tin using a baking paper.

Step 2 - Next, lightly mix in a big mixing bowl the sugar, eggs, oil and canna-oil. Also, you must combine the orange rind, raisins, and grated carrots.

Step 3 - Next, blend the bicarbonate of spices, flour, and soda. At that point, sift into the container. Cautiously combine all the components until you get a smooth touch. It will be a bit bumpy since of the raisins, but you know what I mean.

Step 4 - Pour the mixture into them and bake for 40 to 45 minutes. Nudge the cake with a toothpick to see, in case it is still runny inside. It could come out moist, however make sure is not wet. Calm in the tin for 5 minutes, then turn it out, peel off the paper and let it cool.

Step 5 - Finally, cut into bite-size squares and coat with sugar icing, serve and enjoy!

Chapter 11 – Canna-Cinnabon

Who doesn't like having a lovely Cinnabon roll right? Fine, sure, you could go to your local Cinnabon Bakery. Or, you could get out your kitchen gloves and create these astonishing creamy pleasures that will leave you wanting more and buzz up your whole day!

Preparing Your Canna-Cinnabon:

For this formula, you are going to want a little Canna Milk, therefore here's what you'll want to make the perfect Marijuana milk:

- 1 liter of whole milk, full-fat milk
- 25 grams of your most magnificent buds
- Medium saucepan
- Cheesecloth
- Large mixing bowl

Instructions:

1. In a steel mixing bowl, combine your Marijuana buds with your milk and begin whisking them together.

2. Next, heat a pot to a medium light until boils. Decrease your boiling pot of water to low heat and place the bowl, so that the bottom of the pan touches the hot water inside the container.

3. Slow cook on little light the Milk, while stirring from time to time.

4. Allow the Cannamilk to cook from 30 minutes up to 3 hours, depending on the strength and potency you desire.

5. After ready, strain the mixture through a cheesecloth to remove the excess leaves and buds, and store in the fridge.

Ingredients for your Canna-Cinnabon:

- Dough and a 1/2 cup of warm milk
- 1/2 Cup of Canna milk
- Two eggs
- 1/3 cup of margarine (melted)
- 4 and 1/2 cups of bread flour
- One teaspoon of salt

- 1/2 cup of sugar
- 2 and a 1/2 teaspoons of bread yeast

Cinnamon Sugar Mixture:

- 1 cup of packed brown sugar
- 2 and a 1/2 teaspoons of ground cinnamon
- 1/3 cup of butter - softened preferred

Frosting:

- 1 package of cream cheese – softened preferred
- 1/4 cup of butter - softened preferred
- 1 and a 1/2 cups of powdered sugar
- 1/2 teaspoon of vanilla
- 1/8 teaspoon of salt

Instructions:

Step 1 - I tend to utilize a bread machine for this step as it saves a lot of time. Add directly in all the dough ingredients and start pressing. You need the dough to double in size in the end.

Step 2 - Once it has increased in dimensions, take the dough out of the machine and let it sit, covered on a floured coated surface for about a good 15 minutes. In the time being, blend in a bowl some brown sugar and cinnamon.

Step 3 - Roll the dough into a 16 × 21 inch square, and spread the batter with 1/3 cup of butter, and sprinkle evenly with cinnamon and sugar combination.

Step 4 - Now comes the pleasurable part, starting with a long edge; roll up the dough and then cut into 12 rolls. Put the rolls in a lightly greased 9×13 inch baking pan. Cover and put aside to rise. You need them to double in size.

Step 5 - Bake the rolls in a preheated oven on 400° F until golden brown for about 12 to 15 minutes.

Step 7 - Next, beat together the icing elements and spread frosting on warm rolls in advance of serving, and enjoy!

Chapter 12 - Egg Muffin with Salad

Sunday morning is the most significant time of the week. Once you wake up, there's no stress, and you could spoil yourself with a pleasant Gourmet breakfast, that takes about 15 minutes to make. All right, first and foremost, let's start with the Egg Muffin. For this formula, you are going to need some Marijuana Butter.

Ingredients:

- 3 - 4 Mushrooms
- 2 Slices of Cheese – any Cheese will do
- 1/2 Onion
- 1 Tomato
- 6 - 8 Eggs
- 1/2 teaspoon of Cannabutter

Instructions:

Step 1 - Slice and dice your mushrooms, tomatoes and onions. The idea is to cut them to a small salad like sizes, and the cheese could be sliced into small squares.

Step 2 - Breakdown the eggs into a bowl and mix them. Also, add the mix and Cannabutter till you get a smooth texture.

Step 3 - Next, put them side down on a wire rack and chill in the refrigerator until hardened.

Step 4 - Stripe a muffin's tray with paper cups, and put in each cup an assortment of fillings. For instance, for each muffin, you can fill with mushrooms and cheese. Additionally, you could add extras, and fill them with tomatoes and onion.

Step 5 - Pour the egg mixture into each cup. 3/4 of the container.

Step 6 – Once the preheated oven is about 230 degrees Celsius, start to bake for 10 to 15 minutes. At that point Grill for an extra 5 Minutes.

Step 7 - Serve Hot, and enjoy!

Chapter 13 – Hungry Strawberries

Strawberries are looking delicious, yet why not top them up with some amazing chocolate and take it to the next level by adding a Canna Twist right? Here's my version of Hungry Strawberries. For this formula, you are going to want some Marijuana butter.

Ingredients:

- 16 ounces of milk chocolate chips
- Two tablespoons of shortening
- 1 pound of fresh strawberries with leaves
- Ice-cream - Not essential
- White chocolate - Not essential

Instructions:

Step 1 - First of all, in a double boiler, you should melt the chocolate, shortening a teaspoon of Cannabutter, and frequently stir it till it gets smooth properly.

Step 2 - Next, you must hold the strawberries by the stem, and dip each one in melted chocolate, about three-quarters of the way to the stem.

Step 3 - Next, put the stem side down, on a wire rack and chill in the refrigerator until hardened.

Step 4 - After hardened serve with ice-cream on the side or drizzle on top melted white chocolate.

Step 5 – Serve and enjoy!

Chapter 14 – Oreos with Grass

Who doesn't love Oreos right? Especially if you can get high from it!

Ingredients:

- Cookies
- 1 cup of unsalted butter on room temperature
- 1 cup of granulated sugar
- One egg on room temperature
- One teaspoon of pure vanilla extract
- 2 cups of whole-wheat flour
- ¾ cup of cocoa powder
- 1½ teaspoons of baking powder
- One teaspoon of salt

Filling:

- ½ cup of unsalted butter on room temperature
- One tablespoons of half-and-half
- One tablespoon of melted Cannabutter
- One teaspoon of pure vanilla extract
- Pinch of salt

- 3-3½ cups of powdered sifted sugar

Instructions:

Step 1 - First, cream and mix the butter with granulated sugar until it's thoroughly blended. Add the vanilla and egg, then continue to blend.

Step 2 - Next, in a mixing dish, you need to sift together the cocoa powder, whole-wheat flour, baking powder and salt together. Ensure there are no lumps until all the pieces vanish.

Step 3 - Next, add the sifted blend to the butter mixture, and mix on low speed. Ensure everything is blended, even the bits that stick to the side of the bowl.

Step 4 - Ensure you divide the dough in half, wrap it, then refrigerate for about 1 hour.

Step 5 - Make sure you preheat the oven to about 350 Farenheight, then line a baking sheet with parchment paper, and don't forget to roll out the dough onto a lightly floured surface, and it should be less than ¼-inch thick.

Step 6 - Next, you must cut the shape of your pick and bake for 10 to 13 minutes until set.

For the filling:

After the cookies are baked and cooled, its time for that fantastic filling to be made.

Step 1 - First, you have to combine the butter, half and half, vanilla, canna-butter and salt, till is well joint. Regards to the combination, it will be lumpy, so scrape frequently.

Step 2 - Add sugar, and mix on low speed until it's all mixed well.

Step 3 - After ready, spread the filling on one cookie and cover one another. Serve it and enjoy!

Note: If you've got any leftover, you could save it in a jar for about 15 to 20 days in the fridge.

Chapter 15 – Apple-pHigh

Remember that feeling while you're craving something sweet to eat after you had a joint right? ☺ Well, this recipe isn't for the health conscious Marijuana lovers yet this creamy, delightful treat is sure to get you intense and makes you go wild.

First let's get ready to make a Cheesecake

- 6 cups of thinly sliced apples
- 3/4 cup of white sugar
- One tablespoon of Cannabutter
- One teaspoon of ground cinnamon
- One recipe pass attempt for a 9-inch double-crust pie
- Ice-cream - Optional

Instructions for your Apple-pHigh:

Step 1 - Prepare the slice apples; measured to 6 cups.

Step 2 - In a bowl. mix sugar and cinnamon.

Step 3 - Arrange the apples in layers within the pie plate. Shake on each layer some cinnamon and sugar. Add on the top layer some cannabutter and cover with top crust.

Step 4 - Place on lowest rack in a preheated oven for about 450 degrees F or 230 degrees C. Bake it for 10 minutes, then reduce the oven temperature to 350 degrees F or 175 degrees C and bake it for 30 to 35 minutes longer.

Step 5 - Serve cold or warm with some ice cream, and enjoy!

Chapter 16 - Cinnamon Grass Rolls

Don't you love Cinnamon rolls? Well, imagine an amazing feeling while you are kept energetic all evening. Here's a recipe for the decisive dessert called Cinnamon Grass Rolls, the tastiest of the methods for all Marijuana fans. For this formula, you are going to want a little Cannamilk, so in case you haven't got any, here is how you can make it.

Cannamilk ingridients:

*   1 liter of whole milk or full-fat milk
*   25 grams of your most exceptional Cannabis
*   Medium saucepan
*   Cheesecloth
*   Metal made large mixing bowl
*   Whisk or stirring spoon

Cannamilk Instructions:

1. Put a few inches of water into the medium pot, and put the water on

medium temperature, bringing the liquid to a slight boil.

2. In a steel bowl, combine your Marijuana buds with your milk, and begin whisking them together. This is the fun part.

3. Decrease your boiling pot of water to low heat. Thus the liquid starts to rumble and put the steel bowl so that the bottom of the pan touches the hot water inside the vessel. This will produce a semi-double boiling effect, keeping your milk at a stabilized temperature to prevent it from curdling.

4. Make sure you keep the heat low and slow cook the milk and Cannabis to avert the THC from getting crumbling. Mix it occasionally with your whisk, to keep the mixture combined.

5. Allow the Cannamilk to cook from a minimum of 30 minutes, up to 3 hours, subject on the strength and potency you craving. Make sure that this entire

cook time is happening with a shallow heat.

6. After this prepared, strain the mixture through a cheesecloth to eliminate the buds and leaves, and pile your freshly prepared Cannamilk in the fridge for future usage.

Cinnamon Grass Rolls ingredients:

- One packet of instant yeast
- 3/4 cup of unsweetened almond milk
- 1/4 cup of Cannamilk
- 1/2 cup of vegan butter, separated
- 1/4 tsp of salt
- 3 cups of unbleached all-purpose flour
- 1 - 1/2 tsp of ground cinnamon
- 1/4 cup + 1 Tbsp of organic cane sugar, divided

Cinnamon Grass Rolls instructions:

1. Preheat oven to 350 degrees

2. In the meanwhile, use a large saucepan, heat the almond milk and 3 Tbsp soil

balance until warm and melted, but don't boil it. Take out from heat and let cool down. It could be warm but not too hot. Overheating will destroy the yeast. Relocate it into a large mixing bowl and sprinkle on yeast. Allow activating for 10 minutes. Add 1 Tbsp of sugar and salt, and stir it.

3. Add 1/2 cup of flour at a time, and keep on stirring as you go. The dough will be sticky, but while is thick, relocate it to a lightly floured surface and press for a minute or so, till it forms a loose ball shape. Don't over mix. In the meanwhile, use another mixing bowl, coat with canola or grape seed oil, and add your dough ball back in. Shield with plastic wrap and set aside to rise for about 1 hour long. It could double in dimension.

4. Regards to the floured surface, you should roll out the dough. It could be in a thin box. Brush with 3 Tbsp of melted soil balance and top with 1/4 cup of sugar and 1/2 − 1 Tbsp of cinnamon.

5. Beginning at one end, firmly roll up the dough, and situate seam side down. At that moment with a serrated knife or a string of floss, cut the dough into 1.5 to 2 inch sections, and position in a well-buttered 8×8 inch square or comparably sized round pan. Challenge gently to get out of it as most rolls as likely will be stuck.

6. Brush with the outstanding 2 Tbsp of soil balance, but make sure it's already melted, and shield with a plastic wrap. Next, set on top of the oven or a warm surface to let it rise while you have an advantage.

7. Once the stove is sizzling, bake your rolls for about 25 to 30 minutes, or until is slightly golden brown. Make sure that you allow it to cool for a few minutes and then serve straight away.

8. Now comes the decent part, the Grass Frosting. Create a simple mixture of 1 cup of organic powdered sugar, 1 Tbsp of

Cannamilk, and 1 Tbsp of almond milk. In case you need it stronger add two spoons. Enjoy!

Chapter 17 - Home-produced GrassNog

Who doesn't love some Eggnog right? Well, this is designed to make your holiday season extra happy and keep you vibrant!

Ingredients:

- 2 grams of bud
- 4 cups of milk
- Five whole cloves
- 1/2 teaspoon of vanilla extract
- One teaspoon of ground cinnamon
- 12 egg yolks
- 1 and a 1/2 cups of sugar
- 2 and a 1/2 cups of light rum
- 4 cups of light cream
- Two teaspoons of vanilla extract
- 1/2 teaspoon of ground nutmeg
- Cheese Cloth, or something to strain out the grass.

Instructions:

Step 1 - Mix your grass, milk, cloves, 1/2 teaspoon of vanilla and cinnamon in a saucepan, and heat over a low light roughly 45 minutes. Don't burn the milk, because you need it to be just right. Hot but not too hot!

Step 2 - Now comes the dangerous part, which is to make the egg to your Nogg. In a large dish, combine your egg yolks and sugar. Whip it carefully till it's just about soft. Pour your cannamilk blend gradually into the eggs, while whisking. Put the mixture into the saucepan, and cook over a low-medium light, stirring for 3 minutes, but don't let it boil.

Step 3 - Strain the mixture with your cheesecloth. You don't need any of the leaves in your Nogg, but it's up to you.

Step 4 - Add to your strained mixture rum, cream, two teaspoons of vanilla and nutmeg. You could get pretty original here. Chill overnight.

Step 5 - Pour it into a Cup, serve, and enjoy!

Chapter 18 - New York Cheesecake with Cannabis

There's no healthier way to spice up your evening than with a nice slice of our New York Cheesecake with Cannabis. This formula isn't for the health conscious Marijuana fans, but this creamy appealing treat is guaranteed to get you high and make you go wild. For this great recipe you're going to want a bit of a Cannabutter.

Instructions:

First and foremost, use the cooking ratio as follows: Utilize roughly 1 cup of butter for each ½ ounce of your Cheesecake.

1.   Initiate with spreading your ground chunks, trim or shake equally onto a baking sheet with baking paper, and then preheat your oven to 240 Fahrenheit, and bake it for about 40 to 50 minutes. Your pot will turn out very desiccated. Nevertheless, this is the result you want.

2. In a medium cooking pan, heat 1-2 quarts of water and allow this to get hot. After ready, throw in your sticks of butter, and remember, two sticks for ½ ounce grass. Retain the heat on medium-low to slowly, and melt the butter.

3. After the butter has melted, add in those dank buds you just defined in the oven. Mix the blend continuously, and let it cook on your lowest heat, setting it for 2½ to 3½ hours.

4. After the dough has slow cooked long enough, take a cheesecloth and place it over a bowl sufficiently to hold your butter. Drizzle the combination over the cheesecloth and put it into the bowl carefully. Make sure you wrap the cheesecloth and offer a squeeze to extract any remaining oil.

5. Allow the mixture to cool for about 45 minutes, and then place it in the fridge to cool it a little further. While you put this THC laden concoction in the refrigerator, over time, you will see that the top layer will rise separately from

the water. This is when you are going to peel off after it's detached. Make sure all extra water is scraped off, and store your fresh reefer extract in a jar or air-tight vessel.

Now that we have done our preparation let's begin to make our Cheesecake

Requirements:

- 15 graham crackers, crushed
- One tablespoon of melted butter
- One tablespoon of melted Canna-butter
- Four packages of cream cheese
- 1 - 1/2 cups of white sugar
- 3/4 cup of milk
- Four eggs
- 1 cup of sour cream
- One tablespoon of vanilla citation
- 1/4 cup of all-purpose flour if possible
- A small bar of Dairy milk chocolate or something alike

Instructions to make your Reefer Cake:

1. Heat your oven to 350 degrees, and carefully grease a 9-inch springform pan.

2. Recall that the mixing bowl you got out in the start; and mix you're your graham cracker crumbs with your cannabutter and melted butter. Press the mixture to the bottom of the springform pan.

3. In a different bowl, combine cream cheese with sugar till is even. Blend in milk, and then mix in the eggs one at a time. Blend in vanilla, sour cream, and flour until smooth. Pour filling into prepared crust.

4. Bake in the heated oven for about an hour and switch the oven off, and allow it to cool within the closed oven for about 5 to 6 hours because this will avert cracking. Chill it in the refrigerator.

5. Next, use a small pot over low heat, melt the chocolate properly, and add a bit of cream then stir it till is smooth.

6. Pour on top, or garnish if you prefer, serve, and enjoy!

Chapter 19 - Delirious Chocolate Cookies

You must know that feeling while you're at home on a Sunday afternoon, and suddenly the phone rings... and the next thing you know is that your best friend is coming over right? Well, these Delirious Chocolate Cookies are designed to spice up that Sunday afternoon for sure! Before I get started, for this recipe, you are going to have to make a little Cannamilk.

Cannamilk Ingredients:

- 1 liter of whole milk or full-fat milk
- 25 grams of your highest Cannabis
- Medium saucepan
- Cheesecloth
- Metal large mixing bowl
- Whisk or stirring spoon

Cannamilk Instructions:

1. Put a few inches of water into the medium pot, and put the water on

medium temperature, bringing the liquid to a slight boil.

2. In a steel bowl, combine your Marijuana buds with your milk, and begin whisking them together. This is the fun part.

3. Decrease your boiling pot of water to low heat. Thus the liquid starts to rumble and put the steel bowl so that the bottom of the pan touches the hot water inside the vessel. This will produce a semi-double boiling effect, keeping your milk at a stabilized temperature to prevent it from curdling.

4. Make sure you keep the heat low and slow cook the milk and Cannabis to avert the THC from getting crumbling. Mix it occasionally with your whisk, to keep the mixture combined.

5. Allow the Cannamilk to cook from a minimum of 30 minutes, up to 3 hours, subject on the strength and potency you craving. Make sure that this entire

cook time is happening with a shallow heat.

6.   After this prepared, strain the mixture through a cheesecloth to eliminate the buds and leaves, and pile your freshly prepared Cannamilk in the fridge for future usage.

Delirious Chocolate Cookies Ingredients:

*   1 cup of packed brown sugar
*   1/2 cup of shortening
*   Two squares of unsweetened chocolate, melted
*   One egg
*   1/2 cup of buttermilk, and 1 cup of chopped walnuts - optional
*   1/4 teaspoon of baking soda
*   1/2 teaspoon of salt
*   One teaspoon of vanilla extract

This recipe is quick and straightforward to cook: With only 20 mins You could have these delicious cookies ready for your tea party.

Instructions:

• Heat your oven to 350 degrees Fahrenheit. This is vital, as you want to put the mixture in, while the oven is hot.

• Add your cream brown sugar, shortening, melted chocolate, egg, buttermilk, and cannamilk. I tend to utilize 2/3 buttermilk and a 1/3 cannamilk, but the quantity depends on how strong you need your cookies to be

• Add all other ingredients and beat it until is smooth.

• Drop onto a greased cookie sheet and bake for 12 to 15 minutes, then serve and enjoy!

Chapter 20 - Marijuana Infused Pancakes

Only recently my friend Michelle told me she had gone to her Grandma's house for a delicious Sunday breakfast. She said that she had some delicious Pancakes while she was there. This inspired me to jazz it up a little which is known as Marijuana Infused Pancakes. It's the standard recipe but with a significant twist. For this formula, you will need some canna-oil.

Canna-Oil Ingredients:

•   1-1 ½ ounces of finely ground Cannabis, buds or trim.
•   Twenty-eight ounces of cooking oil, which is always better with olive oil.

Canna-Oil Instructions:

•   First, boil your oil in the saucepan on a low to medium heat. Ensure that it doesn't boil.
•   After hot enough, drop in the 1 to 1 and a ½ ounces of excellent ground Marijuana and stir thoroughly.

- The key here is to mix, so that the oil doesn't get too hot.
- After you have been slow cooking the buds for about 1.5 to 2 hours, take them off the cooktop.
- Drizzle the mixture through a cheesecloth and into the container that you will be keeping your silky Canna-mixture.
- Put the jar of Canna Oil in a dark place or the fridge for storage.

Marijuana Infused Pancakes Ingredients:

- 1 to 1/2 cups of all-purpose flour, 3 and a 1/2 teaspoons of baking powder, one teaspoon of salt and one tablespoon of white sugar.
- 1 and a 1/4 cups of milk, one egg, three tablespoons of butter and make sure it's melted.

Marijuana Infused Pancakes Instructions:

Step 1 - First, use a medium to large size container, sift together the baking powder, the flour, sugar and salt. Create a hole in the center, and dispense inside some milk, egg and melted butter, then mix them until it's flat.

Step 2 - Next, you must heat a lightly oiled griddle or frying pan over medium-high heat. This is where you will utilize your canna-oil btw. Transfer, or scoop the batter onto the grill, and use roughly 1/4 cup for every pancake.

Step 3 - Cook till is brown on both sides and serve it while is hot.
This method goes well with strawberries, or even with ice cream, it's up to you to make it more unique. Enjoy!

Chapter 21 – Tripping Chocolate Pudding

Nothing to a certain extent hits home with a stoner like the mixture of creamy chocolate and fragrant Cannabis. Adore this delicious tripping chocolate Pudding in the vessel with friends or even by yourself alone. This textbook formula brings any 420-friendly meeting or get-together, and a great way to get super baked once you've just enjoyed the perfect dinner. Here's my formula for the ultimate Tripping Pudding, the creamiest of recipes for all Marijuana lovers.

For this formula, you are going to need the magical powers of Cannamilk, a great base to have to lie around for milk-based methods where you need to add in an extra reefer touch.

Cannamilk Ingredients:

- 1 liter of whole milk or full-fat milk
- 25 grams of your highest Cannabis
- Medium saucepan
- Cheesecloth
- Metal large mixing bowl

- Whisk or stirring spoon

Cannamilk Instructions:

1. Put a few inches of water into the medium pot, and put the water on medium temperature, bringing the liquid to a slight boil.

2. In a steel bowl, combine your Marijuana buds with your milk, and begin whisking them together. This is the fun part.

3. Decrease your boiling pot of water to low heat. Thus the liquid starts to rumble and put the steel bowl so that the bottom of the pan touches the hot water inside the vessel. This will produce a semi-double boiling effect, keeping your milk at a stabilized temperature to prevent it from curdling.

4. Make sure you keep the heat low and slow cook the milk and Cannabis to avert the THC from getting crumbling.

Mix it occasionally with your whisk, to keep the mixture combined.

5.   Allow the Cannamilk to cook from a minimum of 30 minutes, up to 3 hours, subject on the strength and potency you craving. Make sure that this entire cook time is happening with a shallow heat.

6.   After this prepared, strain the mixture through a cheesecloth to eliminate the buds and leaves, and pile your freshly prepared Cannamilk in the fridge for future usage.

Tripping Chocolate Pudding Ingredients:

- 3 cups of Cannamilk
- A ½ cup of your favorite cocoa powder
- 12 tablespoons of your preferred sugar
- Four tablespoons of cornstarch
- One teaspoon of vanilla extract
- Whipped cream if desired

This recipe is quick and straightforward to prepare: Only 10 minute cook time, but this formula can serve four people.

Tripping Chocolate Pudding Instructions:

• Blend your sugar, cocoa powder, and cornstarch in a saucepan and then gradually stir in your Cannamilk.
• Bring the combination to a boil and stir regularly.
• Mix for a few more minutes until thick.
• Add in the vanilla after you've turned off the heat, and finally mix them together.
• Put the mixture in a container and chill it to calm.
• Serve up your freshly made Pudding, add whipped cream in case you'd like and enjoy!

Chapter 22 – Hyped Up Strawberry-Banana Smoothie

There's no better way to twitch your morning then a smoothie that will energize and deliver you with a nice dose of marijuana. This formula is for the health conscious Marijuana fans, or somebody who needs a light breakfast drink or a post-lunch nosh. Expand your stoner weekend days on enjoying this appetizingly fruity and ganja filled beverage.

A pitcher serves two people and takes only 10 minutes to prepare and create. Make sure to have your Cannabutter available, as well as a regular blender. In case you have other ingredients you like in smoothies, make sure to add them into this formula to make your Reefer Refresher that much more delightful.

CannaButter Instructions:

First of all, the cooking ratio: Utilize approximately 1 cup of butter for each ½ ounce of Cannabis.

1. Start with spreading your ground nuggets, jiggle or trim equally onto a baking sheet with a baking paper. Heat your oven to 240 Degrees Fahrenheit or 115 Degrees Celsius, and bake it for about 40 to 50 minutes. It will turn out very dry, but this is the result you want.

2. In a medium cooking pan, heat 1-2 quarts of water and allow this to get hot. After ready, throw in your sticks of butter, but remember; two sticks for ½ ounce grass. Retain the heat on medium-low to slowly melt the butter.

3. Subsequently, the butter has melted; add in those dank buds you just defined in the stove. Mixing it regularly, and allow it to cook on your lowest heat setting for 2½ to 3½ hours.

4. After the dough has slow cooked long enough, take a cheesecloth and place it over a bowl substantial sufficient to hold your batch of butter. Dispense the mixture over the cheesecloth and into the pan cautiously. Next, make sure that you wrap the cheesecloth and give

it a squeeze to extract any remaining oil.

5. Allow the mixture to cool for about 45 minutes, and then place it in the fridge to cool a little further. While you put this THC laden concoction in the refrigerator, over time, the top layer will rise separately from the water, and remember that this is the part when you are going to peel off after it's completely separated. Make sure all extra water is scraped off and store your fresh reefer extract in a jar or air-tight container for future usage.

Hyped Up Strawberry-Banana Smoothie Ingredients:

o   Three tablespoons of Cannabutter
o   One frozen banana
o   A ½ cup of frozen strawberries
o   Three tablespoons of shredded coconut
o   ½ cup thin vanilla yogurt
o   ¼ cup coconut or dairy milk
o   A few ice cubes

Hyped Up Strawberry-Banana Smoothie Instructions:

1. Melt your three tablespoons of Cannabutter in a small saucepan on deficient heat. After the butter is liquid, set it aside.

2. Put your strawberries, banana, yogurt, shredded coconut, and milk into a blender, and pour the three tablespoons of melted Cannabutter over the elements. Combine on medium-high power, or until flat.

3. Add in the ice cubes and blend until you've produced the smoothie consistency that you desire.

4. After your Reefer Refresher is prepared, dispense it in a glass and relish your weekend by yourself or with friends. This is a delightful way to get your light buzz of Marijuana for the morning, therefore don't miss out on this gentle and energizing formula! Enjoy!

Chapter 23 - Extreme Breakfast with Marijuana Milk

Health is a vital part of everyday well-being, but it doesn't mean you have to give up being a stoner to stay healthy. There are so many ways to include Marijuana into your daily diet, even if case you're cleansing your body and consuming nutrient-rich plates. Relish this blazing superfood breakfast bowl, crowded with vitamins and minerals from organic and robust components, varied with your favorite reefer straining. Get to your local farmer's market or health food grocery store and start arranging this illuminating dish that is sure to bring you energy through your day! For this ganja breakfast, you'll want to have a bit of a freshly made Marijuana Milk. You can do this with coconut milk, or with dairy.

Cannamilk ingridients:

- 1 liter of whole milk or full-fat milk
- 25 grams of your most exceptional Cannabis
- Medium saucepan
- Cheesecloth

- Metal made large mixing bowl
- Whisk or stirring spoon

Cannamilk Instructions:

1. Put a few inches of water into the medium pot, and put the water on medium temperature, bringing the liquid to a slight boil.

2. In a steel bowl, combine your Marijuana buds with your milk, and begin whisking them together. This is the fun part.

3. Decrease your boiling pot of water to low heat. Thus the liquid starts to rumble and put the steel bowl so that the bottom of the pan touches the hot water inside the vessel. This will produce a semi-double boiling effect, keeping your milk at a stabilized temperature to prevent it from curdling.

4. Make sure you keep the heat low and slow cook the milk and Cannabis to avert the THC from getting crumbling.

Mix it occasionally with your whisk, to keep the mixture combined.

5. Allow the Cannamilk to cook from a minimum of 30 minutes, up to 3 hours, subject on the strength and potency you craving. Make sure that this entire cook time is happening with a shallow heat.

6. After this prepared, strain the mixture through a cheesecloth to eliminate the buds and leaves, and pile your freshly prepared Cannamilk in the fridge for future usage.

After your Cannamilk is prepared, grip a blender and collect the following components. This formula serves 2 and takes only 20 minutes to make, blend and pour.

Extreme Breakfast with Marijuana Milk Ingredients:

*   1½ cups of Cannamilk
*   One medium to large avocado – skinless

- Two packets of frozen acai puree
- One scoop of your favorite protein or supplement powder mix
- One mango - diced
- Two bananas

For Toppings:

- Two tablespoons of raw hemp seed
- One tablespoon of raw chia seeds
- Chopped walnuts
- One tablespoon of bee pollen
- Two tablespoons of granola
- One tablespoon of torn coconut
- Some garden-fresh seasonal berries

Extreme Breakfast with Marijuana Milk Instructions:

This part is straightforward.

Step 1 - Add your bananas, avocado, protein powder, and mango, into a blender. Dispense the 1½ cup of Cannamilk over the ingredients.

Step 2 - Blend until even.

Step 3 - Decant in a bowl and top off with your choice of toppings, the list above can give you specific concepts. Add as much or as few as you wish.

Relish the high of healthy consumption, food that brings you energy and motivation, while experiencing the euphoric effects of your favorite Marijuana strain.

Let your wake and bake to be an inspirational one by kicking your morning off with this Extreme Breakfast with Marijuana Milk. Enjoy!

Bonus Chapter - Thai Stir Fry Canna Veggie

This Thai Stir Fry Canna Veggie has all the aromatic medical Marijuana you need, including; some delightful rice noodles, freshly cut veggies and some sweet sauce. This formula is a quick cook and is perfect for inviting your vegan friends to have a great time together.

Ingredients:

- One pack of Thai glass noodles
- One head of broccoli
- One bag of bean sprouts
- One shallot finely chopped
- One spring onion finely chopped
- Six small shiitake mushrooms sliced
- 12 ounces of green beans
- 2-3 handfuls of fresh basil
- Red chili sauce
- A ¼ cup of Canna-Oil
- 3 to 4 teaspoons of soy sauce
- Paprika to taste
- Sage
- Pepper
- Chilli flakes
- One tablespoon of lime juice

- 2 ounces of sesame oil

Canna-Oil Ingredients:

- 1-1 ½ ounces of finely ground Cannabis, buds or trim.
- Twenty-eight ounces of cooking oil, which is always better with olive oil.

Canna-Oil Instructions:

- First, boil your oil in the saucepan on a low to medium heat. Ensure that it doesn't boil.
- After hot enough, drop in the 1 to 1 and a ½ ounces of excellent ground Marijuana and stir thoroughly.
- The key here is to mix so that the oil doesn't get too hot.
- After you have been slow cooking the buds for about 1.5 to 2 hours, take them off the cooktop.
- Drizzle the mixture through a cheesecloth and into the container that you will be keeping your silky Canna-mixture.
- Put the jar of Canna-Oil in a dark place or the fridge for storage.

Instructions:

Step 1 - Boil a medium sized pot of water.

Step 2 - After the water is boiling, put your pack of Thai rice noodles into the hot water, and start stirring the noodles regularly.

Step 3 - Around 10 minutes later, your noodles are prepared. Grab a strainer and drain the water.

Step 4 - Take hold of a wok or large frying pan and turn the stove up to medium heat, while pour in your ¼ cup of Canna-Oil.

Step 5 - Next, cut your vegetables and put them to cook into the wok.

Step 6 - Enhance your vegetables to the wok or frying pan after your Canna-Oil has warmed up.

Step 7 - Start to stir the veggies. Thus they become coated equally in that good Canna-Oil.

Step 8 - After the vegetables are cooked and become a little crispy, add in your boiled noodles, your soy sauce, lime juice, sesame oil, chili sauce, and spices.

Step 9 - Add in your fresh basil last, so that it won't wilt. Cook the noodles and vegetables for around 5 to 10 minutes longer, and your dish ready to go.

Step 10 - Serve and enjoy!

About Marie Spilotro

Marie was born and raised in California. As a child, Marie spent lots of time in the kitchen, but soon realized that she want to become a professional Chef for life.

Marie was a great student while she attended at The Art of Institute of California in San Diego, where she received her diploma.

Even though received her education, she wanted to learn more from the most famous cousins around the World, so decided on a travel plan for an official visit of; UK, France and Italy.

Marie has managed to visit, London, Liverpool, Manchester, Paris, Nice, Marseille, Rome, Venice and Pachino.

Pachino in Sicily was a very significant part of Marie's travels, because she not only found the most famous tomato there is, but the love of her life, Frank.

Marie's main interest in Pachino was to taste one of the most famous tomato on the world, called "Pomodoro di Pachino", yet she fallen love in Frank Spilotro.

They got married and moved back to California together where they both specializing in a field of Cannabis Cultivation, including indoor, outdoor and greenhouse gardening of medical cannabis.

CPSIA information can be obtained
at www.ICGtesting.com
Printed in the USA
LVHW012346230520
656396LV00004B/170